Every Little Thing:

Small Breakthroughs, Big Mistakes, Endless Lessons

Essays

Also by Mary Lou Sanelli:

FICTION

The Star Struck Dance Studio of Yucca Springs

NONFICTION

Among Friends
A Woman Writing
Falling Awake

POETRY

Small Talk
Craving Water
The Immigrant's Table
Women in the Garden
Close at Hand
Long Streaks of Flashing Daylight
Lineage

BOOKS FOR CHILDREN

Bella Likes to Try (forthcoming)

Every Little Thing:

*Small Breakthroughs, Big Mistakes,
Endless Lessons*

Essays

by

Mary Lou Sanelli

CHATWIN BOOKS
Seattle

paperback ISBN 978-1-63398-135-5

Cover design by Rigoli Creative

Interior design by Vladimir Verano, Vertvolta Design

Dedication:

For Larry, for every kindness, every encouragement. Basically, for everything.

For Ken Lambertson my greatest father figure.

For the editors of my columns where many of these writings originated, every one of you has saved me from feeling as though my work is irrelevant—even if it only feels this way. Thank you for giving my thoughts a voice for so many years. Thank you. Thank you. Thank you.

Most of all, thank you to all who live in Seattle. Some of the recent changes here have not been easy to endure, I know, but they have wedged another kind of city open, and a lot of new and better things have come in, too.

Contents

INTRODUCTION:
ON BECOMING A WRITER

WHEN I WAS IN THE THIRD GRADE, I wore a retainer. My words came out thick, like how they sound now whenever, unwisely, I drink that second glass of wine.

Adding insult to injury, my family moved out of the city, and I suddenly found myself living in a small New England town, surrounded not by other Italian kids, but by a swirl of "Goldilocks" as my friend Bonnie liked to call them, even though most of the girls were more brunette than blonde. But they had already perfected the art of flinging their bangs, as if each strand was luminous as Marilyn Monroe's. And, heaven forbid, my own frizzy hair was nearly black.

I hid my retainer in my lunch box before I even got to the bus stop.

And I began to sense that if I didn't speak, I could sort of fit in, realizing that I was capable of silence, a total disconnection from everything and everyone I knew at home. It was not my nature, but I could at least *try* to press my lips together and say nothing.

Until I felt a panicky frustration that had to come out somewhere.

Once I left school, I would run, not walk, from the bus stop to my room. Like a friend who listened without making fun, the likes of which I couldn't find at school, my diary—a pale pink journal my mother bought because it was "pretty"—let me express my confusion about adjusting to a new school, a new teacher, a new *life*.

And I continued this way, privately, because everything felt more bearable once I shut the door, sat, and wrote it down.

Eventually these pages became my "journal" and later my "notebook," but even in my teens I was not thinking about becoming a writer. I had no idea that all the time I spent writing had any connection to "becoming a writer." No one I knew was a writer. My parents were not educated people.

What I did know was that as soon as I picked up my pen, my fears settled down. And by the time I finished writing to myself, I felt calmed by the process. And later, at the dinner table (though my family still called it "supper") if someone remembered to ask me how my day had gone, I could answer "fine"—and almost mean it.

Now, when I read one of my earliest entries—like when the popular clique put Curl Free in my locker, or the crush I had on Steven R. that made me start off by saying, "You're going to think I'm crazy, diary, but I LOVE him!"—I can see how I was beginning to understand that life at school would get better, or it wouldn't, but if I could confront my feelings about it, I'd at least have a fighting chance.

These days, whenever I'm asked how I began writing, I say that I owe my writing life to my diary, the blog of my day.

Except it wasn't a blog. I was not writing for an audience. With no pressure to boast or perform, no photos to post, I was writing only for myself. *To* myself. This is how I learned to listen to what my mind had to say.

Which is what I said in a roundabout way on my last book tour to a woman at Bloomsbury Books in Ashland, Oregon when she asked if she needed an agent to get her book "into the universe."

"What is your book about?" I asked.

"Sacred sound devotional chanting circles."

I suddenly felt very square, very *un*-New Age. I wondered if maybe there is a little too much lithium in the Lithia water the town is famous for. I did manage to say, "I think whenever you combine what you love to do with what you know *how* to do, the cross-pollination tells a great story." Which did not even come close to answering her question, I know, but I think every author stumbles through the Q & A in their own best way.

But I could not wait to whip out my tiny notebook and scribble down what she had said. In the same way I couldn't wait to get home from school to write about the time the heaviest girl in our gym class put the meanest one in her place by saying, "My butt may be big, but it will never be as big as your mouth!"

This is why I love to write about real life. I love the stories that come from real people. I could never dream up the woman in Ashland.

Thankfully, I didn't have to.

She was right there.

And she was stunning.

Essays: 2015–2021

"Set wide the window. Let me drink the day."

–Edith Wharton, 1909

FALLING INTO THE NEW YEAR

IT FEELS STRANGE TO PRONOUNCE a new year for the first time. I tend to emphasize the digits as if I can't quite believe in the way they sound.

I woke last night with a pressing thought: *how scary the future feels. It does not make sense. Am I missing something? Testosterone, maybe?*

So scary, in fact, that when I look out the window and see a crow staring back, I am sure it is a sign. Crows do not typically land on my sill, but this one turns its head from side to side, slowly, as if it, too, wants to stress something *it* does not quite believe is true.

I take a deep breath. "Don't look at me like that." I say. "I drank the hard stuff last night and I should never drink the hard stuff. I'm not wired for it."

The crow flies off.

There's really no point in defending yourself to a crow. They bear only truth. And so, I let the truth come: *I am scared to tackle another book. I haven't forgotten what it's like. I am afraid to begin again.*

It can take a lifetime to admit your greatest fear to yourself.

Still, you would think I'd be more confident by now, convinced that I can refine the tone, the phrasing, the pauses, even with the headachy effect of a New Year's gathering that was really more of a Moving Away gathering because my friend is off to live on the Arizona desert. "I'm so over this," he said, meaning long wet winters and it doesn't really matter that he has tried to leave Seattle twice before—this time I believe him.

And since his party felt like the official end of the holidays, first I fell in love with a chilled gimlet—fresh lime, plenty of vitamin C—and then with the music in the background, managing, thanks to gimlet number two, to outlast the only other dancer on the floor, him (he still holds it against me, I think), just to prove that I can still dance until the wee hours. And this was before Prince's *Kiss* came on.

It doesn't take much, a little music, a little alcohol, and poof, I need to dance. When I read that Friedrich Nietzsche, the German philosopher and poet, said he could only believe in a God who would get up and dance, I felt like *my* interpretation of the divine was finally in print for the whole world to see.

I know a longing to dance does not move everyone, but the urge is insistent in me. Even if everyone else stays seated, I try to tap into the part of my brain that does not care what anyone thinks. I give in to the music. To the way my body feels when it expresses the music. This is how I live most true to myself.

But it doesn't keep me from making a complete ass of myself sometimes.

By gimlet number three, I looked around in hopes that no one had seen my fall, or if they had, they saw it as I did: entirely the fault of the slippery floor.

It's not hard to reconstruct what happened. I tried to execute a pirouette.

A *pirouette*!

Feet firmly planted in fifth position; it began well enough. Then suddenly my balance was not balanced anymore.

Earlier, I had debated whether my friend should mix me another. His reason for giving in was simple. He was smart enough to know my hangover would be far worse than any reproach from him. I thanked him. I thanked *me*. Then I made my way back to the dance floor.

And because it's often true that bad decisions make good stories down the line, if not one other embarrassment comes to mind, ever, I think I could write for weeks just by reliving this one. Not that my legs flew up in the air or anything. All in all, it was a pretty graceful landing. A dancer learns how to fall with some degree of dignity.

Even so, it was humiliating.

Wait. I almost forgot. Something else threw me last night. Not to the floor but throw me it did: A friend tapped me on the shoulder and said. "I used to be a man."

"What did you just say?"

She lifted her shoulders and let them drop.

My first thought was *there are no masculine traits to your features, none whatsoever*. I did not say that, of course, only that a person's sexual identity has never been the most interesting thing about them, not to me anyway.

In any case, my friend used to be a man and that's that. I was taken aback, we laughed our tipsy heads off, and we went about our business. She is still someone I will call for an honest opinion. She is interesting. She is interested. She asks questions. She wants to know. Nothing about our friendship will change all that much. She still better never lie to me, come on to my husband, be late one too many times, or borrow money and forget to pay it back. I put both my hands on her shoulders and told her as much.

"Got it," she said.

I wish I could believe that we can ever really know someone, but too much has happened over the years to convince me otherwise. I think our friends are revealed to us slowly, maybe not as slowly as we are revealed to ourselves, but there are slow burning secrets to everyone's story—hers, mine, yours—and one of the hardest choices for a writer is deciding which ember to fan.

Or maybe I am too easily distracted, I don't know.

Like right now. If I walk into the kitchen to pour myself another cup of coffee, I'd better not stare too long at my mother's floral serving platter, I can tell you that. It's mine now, the platter, which means it is propped up on the counter and seldom used. But when I look at it, I mean really look at it, I better have the heart to be swept back into high school.

Possibly I was headed there anyway, since remembering is easier than writing.

Actually, anything is easier than writing.

I was brave in high school, braver than I am now. In my yearbook, there is a photo of me sitting on top of my locker flashing a peace sign at the principal. My first sit-in.

Little has changed. Peace is what I long for and war is what we get.

I'll never forget how my mother used to ring the dinner bell to summon my sisters and me from wherever in the neighborhood we had wandered off to. The bell was loud, too, but it never stopped her from yelling "SUPPER!" at the top of her lungs, even though she could see us running for our lives toward home.

She was just like that. As if before we even sat down she wanted to speed things along, annoyed by how slow family life can be. Though she would never admit it. The one time I tried to talk to her about it she said, "That is not true."

"But I'm the same way, mom. I had to get it from someone."

"I guess we remember things differently," she said with a look that said one more question from me would be one too many.

What she did enjoy was the creative side, peeling the garlic until her fingers reeked, sautéing the cloves with basil and oregano. But waiting for three kids and a husband to polish it off? No. I don't think so.

Consequently, I have long admired people who know how to live more patiently through the crises and chaos of adulthood. My mother could not teach me this skill, sad fact.

She taught me other things, though. Like how thoughts come to us a lot like making a lasagna: layer upon layer upon layer. And that it is important to forgive yourself for making a mistake.

Wait. I don't even know why I thought of that just now. I wasn't even talking about mistakes. Well, maybe *hers*. But it's not like I make all that many.

Shudder.

Okay, any mistakes I make along the way—and I will likely make plenty because I say and do regrettable things when I'm nervous—will hopefully prove that I am, at least, still trying.

It's such a delicate balance, though, vigilance vs. patience. What it takes to make things happen opposed to what it takes to not go crazy while waiting for things to happen.

Oh, the thoughts I pared back today have been cathartic. Nearly as cathartic as dancing was last night. I feel my fears (the worst of them, anyway) slip from my shoulders like pasta sliding off my mother's platter.

I have hung in there.

I have found the courage to begin again.

First Valentine

It was all about "the holidays" for a while, and that's always a crazy time.

Then, a record snowstorm, a rare, white, front, and it was all anyone could talk about. I mean, people *died*.

Eventually, the weather eased.

But we can never look at things exactly how we did before a storm. They press us to weigh certain things. Like readiness, for one. And maybe they even slow us down long enough to consider whether we are satisfied, things of that nature.

I really do have to remind myself to slow down, to let my mind drift, to listen to the birdsong, the waves, the wind. It's why I ride a bicycle. And though the freedom of riding started when I was a kid, only does it dawn on me that all those miles I pedaled led me to a lifelong desire for more.

More distance. More wonder. More awe.

And yet, my first memory of "more" did not begin with my Schwinn, but with those small, sugary, engraved hearts that mark the beginning of February. Somehow, I got the impression that if I collected enough of them, the world would hold a clear and simple message for me, too. Even now, I pinch a few, but in my mind's eye I see myself scooping the entire stash and filling my pockets.

Be Mine. True Love. You Rock.

It's funny because I don't have any reaction whatsoever to fall's candied corn. I suppose sweets are a lot like people. We connect with some and not with others.

And since we had to hand out valentines even to the kids we didn't like, those soppy hearts can still raise a few things about love's duplicity. I can't help but ask myself *whose love is there for me no matter what*?

Whose isn't?

And why not? What happened?

I lean forward over the keyboard . . .

Okay then. When my friend Pummi told me that my smile lines were getting "really bad," for months I didn't want to see her. I didn't want to be reminded that my usual way of moving through life as a younger woman was no longer possible.

It wasn't the first time she'd inspected my face.

She was never cruel, but she acted as if she knew more about aging than I did. And there was something slightly disapproving in her eyes, that was the worst of it. I think she is more worried about aging than she lets on. So, she examines *me*.

And I'm human. I get my feelings hurt.

Still, our job as friends is to forgive. So, I forgive you, Pummi.

Or I *plan* on forgiving you.

We can't force forgiveness, I know this. It takes its sweet time. Then, if you are courageous—that is, courageous enough to have the gut-wrenching conversation about why your feelings were hurt in the first place—you may even find each other again.

I Miss You. Old Friend. I'll Be Calling You Soon.

No sooner do I let this apology out when another love story surfaces. This time, a man fills my thoughts.

Not just any man. Dad.

On the morning of our wedding, the overcast we'd hoped would burn off swelled into the kind of drizzle that can make pulling off a celebration on a shoestring budget (Larry and I insisted on paying for everything ourselves) feel even more overwhelming. I worried that the sky would turn into a downpour or, worse, sprinkle all day.

My dad took one look at me staring upwards, and an even longer look at Larry—both of us a little scruffy to someone from a more formal school of wedding appropriateness—until his eyes, spanning the historic Dungeness Schoolhouse we'd rented, spied the keg of beer in the corner. He looked back at me as if he might want to say something, but he never did. He just crossed the room, got into his rental car, and drove off. If it hadn't been my wedding day, I might have found it disconcerting to watch him flee.

An hour later he was back. I remember thinking I should just be happy he was sober.

Soon, bottles of vodka, gin, scotch, plus every mixer imaginable, were aligned next to the wedding cake. No one can look at my dad and not see raw energy just waiting to be tapped. Tending bar was the place he felt useful. "You think Italians can have a wedding without an open bar?" he asked, but it wasn't really a question. And he winked after he said it, which was unquestionably the greater gift.

As far back as I can remember, I've been a sucker for one of his winks. They didn't come often, but when they did, it was like the sky opening. I will remember *that* wink until the day I die.

My friends, used to cheap beer and homegrown marijuana, wasted no time snuggling up to the bar. We formed a conga line, three steps forward and a kick, three steps back and a kick, that's how much fun our wedding was.

Kisses. Sweetheart. Soul Mate.

Next morning, the schoolhouse manager called to say the floor was caving in. I covered my mouth with my hand, but a smile grew behind my fingers. But even if he'd come to our door, I don't think he would have been able to *tell* I was happy.

I was only twenty-one. No smile lines yet.

As a wedding present, my father gave us enough cash to "get busy," neither too much as to make Larry uncomfortable, nor too little to make me so. Because an immigrant's belief in cold hard cash is legendary and I'd grown up with it.

Save Cash. Buy with Cash. Show Your Love with Cash.

Oh, Pummi?

Miss You. Call Me. We Work. We'll Figure It Out.

Remembering the (Almost) Tsunami

My mother married a man who lived on the island of Oahu.

In a photo I have we are smiling for the camera in a beachfront restaurant. My stomach tightens when I think of those early annual visits to the island when, thrilled to escape Seattle in winter, I would bask in the sun and try to convince myself that I hadn't spent the last thirty years gritting my teeth whenever we spent time together. Lily Tomlin said that "forgiveness means giving up all hope for a better past". Every time I read that line, I want to add *with your mother* as the last three words. It's why the photo comforts me. It shines a little light on mother/daughter love. It shows me a time when we were able to relax with each other, the tension gone, the tropical-sun making everything in the world seem brighter: the palm trees, the bougainvillea, our smiles silently but willingly uniting us.

But life has stages.

Natural, surprising, stages.

Soon after her husband's death, she, too, started to weaken.

When I visited in 2011, I knew that I would have to stay. I was needed. It might have been her shockingly small apartment, or the terrible smell coming from the fridge, or the way she could no longer walk without a great deal of concentration, but it all felt like silent acknowledgment of *it's time, I need you.* I saw it in her eyes.

It was a look that can make a daughter weep.

And it did. I walked into the bathroom and locked the door. Tears ran like rivers down my cheeks.

Once she was gone, only then could I begin to savor the privilege of having helped someone you love to pass on. And in the weeks while we were both letting go of each other, *and* a few tightly held secrets ("I don't think I've ever had an orgasm," she said one day out of the blue), I clung to my new relationship to the island. I called it "falling in love." Which sounds utterly cliché. But what makes me still want to say it is that it holds no pretense for me. It *fits.*

But even if 2011 doesn't hold such a personal memory for you, it is still difficult to recall the year without remembering one date in particular, March 11th, the day all of Hawaii and the West Coast of America waited for a tsunami to roll across the Pacific from Japan.

I still rely on the words "cramped" and "uncomfortable" to describe trying to sleep that night near the top of Wa'ahila Ridge. A friend in Seattle told me she still has trouble visualizing Hawaii without seeing me curled up on the backseat of my car.

At the time, my internal clock had not yet adopted the tempo of everyday life in Hawaii, and along with it, a heightened sense of currents, both air and sea, so that a lot of the time I still felt like I was on vacation, not in a hurry to do anything.

So when the most powerful earthquake ever to hit Japan stunned the world, I was sitting in a waterfront lounge at the far end of Kalakaua Avenue, sipping a Chi Chi Colada, remembering how my mother had called the drink "sunset in a glass," and how I'd rolled my eyes. I'd started to roll my eyes at all the ridiculous things people say to sell the *idea* of Hawaii, but her smile made her face seem softer, less exhausted by the tedious work of packing up one life and moving on to another, and now I close my eyes just *aching* to remember that smile.

The spooky sound of a tsunami siren brought everyone back to reality. Bullhorns warned us to move to upper floors. I ran to my room, packed a bag, nosed my car out of the garage and made a run for the ridge.

Or, rather, a crawl. A long line of traffic inched toward higher ground.

If you have ever flown over the island of Oahu you may remember the Ko'olau Mountain Range that divides the leeward side from the vast, open ocean beyond. The first time I hiked up, the sight of the most isolated island chain in the world was like seeing some new facet of remoteness that had never occurred to me before, like viewing transcendence.

Or, what I think of when I think of the word *transcendence.*

But what also becomes apparent—chillingly so—is that the entire southeast coastline is a plane of low-lying land, as flat as, *gulp,* Fukushima.

Locals and tourists live parallel lives. There is little common ground. There are, however, two things that always seem to bridge the gap: music and food. That night on the ridge top, sitting on tailgates, local people strummed ukuleles and guitars, told stories, fired up BBQ's, divvied up boxes of malasadas, passing one to me, the "skinny Ha'ole lady," and poked fun at each other as we took turns walking off to pee into the dark fringes off the road.

One man recalled the last tsunami set off by an earthquake in Chile. "I run to my truck, no pants. My wife kept yelling, 'where your pants at? Where your pants at?'"

Everyone laughed.

I know this all sounds rather festive for an evening fraught with worry. But I have come to believe that a power greater than the strongest tsunami always works to restore us to the basic human level of caring for one another, and that island life is a whole lot kinder and more enjoyable when you have others to take to the ridges with. I think this is what people really mean when they describe living with aloha.

When the coast was clear, I said to one woman how I hoped I'd see her again, and she looked at me and said, "Next earthquake, we go fo' party here, yah?"

I weighed the prospect of returning to the ridge, which I welcomed, against the likelihood of returning after another tsunami, which I hope never happens. I waved and drove off, winding my way back down to the leeward shore—better known to the world as Waikiki. Where tourists don't pay too much attention to the mountains behind the high-rise hotels unless a rainbow shimmers in a web of sun, water, and air.

And because I'll always be somewhat of a tourist myself (the monetary intricacies of life never let up, and sometimes our careers are dependent on the contacts we made in the earliest stages of it, so that I must work diligently in Seattle to afford time in Hawaii, which has got to be *the* height of first world problems), I like to remember how it felt to flee from where another tsunami can, and likely will, converge one day.

Now when I go to the beach, I like to turn my towel away from the waves so that my view is of the ridges. And I am almost tempted to tell someone visiting the island what it was like up there in 2011 when the roads filled with carloads of people trying to outrun a swelling sea. Until I remember that a vacation and what it could unexpectedly become is not a great icebreaker. Fearing a wave is too far a leap from splashing in one. Danger is one of the hardest things to swallow about paradise.

And if a hurricane is predicted I act like a local now, as though it's no big deal. Because ninety-nine percent of the time it isn't.

But I can't help but look up at the ridges the way the earliest explorers must have stared at them, with pause and respect. I close my eyes and I am back up there trying to sleep with my legs hanging out the car window while hundreds of others keep driving up, and a dog barks from somewhere deep in the valley.

Until, hours later, it's a slow crawl down.

A Blue House

THE COLOR IS THE MOST OBVIOUS difference. It is not white or beige or brown.

It is blue.

Not a brilliant shade of blue, but softer, more inviting, less typical. The blue Goethe was after, I think, when he described blue as a contradiction between excitement and repose.

It is also the largest house on the block. But it doesn't try to rule in any way. Which is not always easy. And a particularly good sign.

I walk closer.

Some would say the lawn needs mowing. To me it feels like a yard that can *breathe*. One of many classics in Seattle, it's the storybook likeness of a country cottage. I have to fight the urge to step up to the front door and ask if I can come inside. I am a little irrational about a house that isn't mine.

Love is like this. *Possessive.*

My friend Lynn has a different reaction to the color. "It's *too* blue," she says.

I think what she means is that the blue reminds her of the postcards from Maui we both received from a mutual friend who will do just about anything to escape winter around here. Right after Lynn received hers she called me, "As *if*," she cried, "anyone around here wants to see sunlight turned up a notch when we're forced to flick on the house lights at three in the afternoon."

I understood. Any reminder of sunshine in January can almost seem cruel, and Lynn is struggling to remain in the city. Days are too short to add daydreaming to the list of things we need to get done before sunset. We can't afford to dream in blue right now. Blue is too far off. Gray is what we have, we can't see past it. We aren't getting through customs or airport security. We are just getting through. Until spring.

But here is a happy thought: the crocuses are up!

Next, the trillium, cut back to nothing last fall.

I tell Lynn that my postcard makes my throat constrict at the thought of swimming in the ocean again. "Oh, I hear you," she says. "I'm from Florida, *hello*." We are both so over the Queen Anne Pool. Laps don't suit either one of us.

And it's not only because of the lecherous man (you know who you are) who stands with his outstretched arms resting on the edge of the pool, not swimming, just standing, ogling as we surface, it's the smell. It always feels good to get into the water, but just as good to leave those bleachy fumes behind.

As soon as this thought is out, I'm reminded of how good it feels to sink into the clean, fresh, *blueblueblue* of sea water. Its silence possibly the only silence left.

It has been a terrible thing to give up on the idea of silence.

Do you remember when it was easier to find? When walking on the beach would ensure it. How, other than the sound of waves breaking, or gulls in concert, the anticipation of silence is what brought you to the shore in the first place. Before cell phones became a way of life, the rest of us forced to listen.

Oh, this search for the perfect home to retreat to.

It isn't just that I love the house and the yard around the house. It isn't just the color, either. It's that when I stand in front of it, I feel as though I belong to the world and I'm safe from it at the same time.

Well, as long as I'm daydreaming . . . my next home (that I *will* find) will have a small terrace perched over the sea. And cell phones (and little yappy dogs) are not allowed—mostly.

I like to imagine a place still capable of this.

CAUSE CÉLÈBRE

IT HAPPENED LAST NIGHT. I was sitting alone in a restaurant. A man asked to join me.

"No, thank you," I said, kindly as I could.

I often travel alone, so it's nothing for me to dine alone, even on a Saturday night.

Even in a small town.

Even in *Wenatchee.*

The man jutted his chin toward my empty chair. "So, who's going to sit here?"

"No one."

He cast me a sneer. "Women your age shouldn't be so picky."

I felt my face heat up.

I stared at him for a moment.

Whatever I say now, I thought, he will answer with an even more insulting jibe. I picked up my wine glass and took a long slow sip. And then I found the words. "For a man with a belly big as yours, you assume a lot about women."

It may not sound like a big deal, but to me it was. The speed at which I connected my thoughts to my voice was worth the awkwardness I had to face—worth more, actually—if I needed to use the bathroom (he sat by the door) or leave (since the door to the bathroom was about two feet from the exit).

I meet women all the time who know exactly how to speak their mind, but I have waited my whole life to be able to deliver the perfect comeback. It has always been a secret desire of mine to know just how to raise my jaw with a tilt of my head until I know just what to say. And how to say it.

At last, I have my own back.

All along, all I had to do was say how I felt. But as a younger woman, it wasn't only that I would go blank inside, disarmed by my own clumsiness, I did not have the patience or the wherewithal to wait a few seconds before shooting back. I did not have the nerve.

I remember the exact morning, not too long ago—after a phone call from a particularly rude editor—when I decided I would no longer take an insult quietly. I was chewing a corner of English muffin, lots of olive oil dripping through my fingers, and along with the Extra Virgin, another lipid slid in, it just did, an essential structural component that might as well have said, "All these years of faking it, taking it, smiling when you should have said, *you fucking idiot. Who do you think you are?*"

Still, I can't imagine why I went so low. I didn't have to pick on the man's belly. I could have left the belly out of it. My own lovely husband has a bit of one himself and I know how he struggles with it.

Wait, I do know why. To aim *below* the belt, just as he had.

Plus, I saw in him the kind of man I have seen quite enough of lately: a man in love with his own ignorance, who snorts when he laughs at women but secretly lives in fear of us and tries to mask it with too much bravado, too much comb over, rejected one too many times (go figure), so that now he wants to throw the first punch whenever possible.

So, I punched back.

Of course, keeping the punch to myself will be impossible. Impossible! And likely to intensify as I re-tell, re-live, re-tell, re-*live*.

Already my writing mind is losing focus. It wants to pick up the phone. It wants to tell someone what happened. It wants to reveal how I dealt with a punch, how I felt afterward. It wants to celebrate!

I hope a lot of you will appreciate my cause célèbre. You may even say to yourself, "I know just what you mean."

Because you do. You know exactly how important this passage is, what an accomplishment it can feel like.

What a feat.

Two Steps

May is not simply a month. It marks the beginning of recital season, when students of all disciplines do not look at the world through the eyes of children, but through the eyes of performers, picturing themselves as skilled and confident as their supportive parents had hoped they could be.

That is the best-case scenario, anyway.

There is always the exception.

Last week I met another sort of parent altogether. She wasn't as irritating as, say, a reality TV mom, but she was just as upsetting. I was warming up in my studio when she opened the door a crack to ask if her daughter could watch. They were from Beijing, she said. Together they felt smaller than I am. Such delicate carriage.

We talked briefly about classes. And when she said, "I don't think my daughter is pretty enough to be a dancer, her hands and feet are too ugly," she looked at me expectantly as if waiting for my agreement. The warm feeling I'd had quickly chilled, as though clouds passed over the sun. Not sure what to do, or why she'd say such a thing, I decided not to call further attention to her remark.

Anyone new to a dance studio is generally wide-eyed, and this girl was no exception. There is a positive charge that comes from connection to other dancers and I couldn't imagine what her mother thought she was accomplishing by trying to suppress it. It all happened so quickly, but it triggered something in me more lasting: the idea that anyone—even a parent, especially a parent—has the right to quash a child's confidence, well, that will never sit right with me.

It's my studio, I thought, *so this will end my way.* I knelt down, looked directly into the girl's eyes and said, "You have the loveliest hands and feet. If you choose to dance, you will be an amazing, talented, beautiful dancer."

Her mother was aghast, and her face showed it. She shook her head "no."

I nodded, "yes."

By the hand, she led her daughter out of my studio.

Why on earth had they come?

I ran to the window to watch them walk across the parking lot. It was clear the mother was speaking. Remembering what my friend Yvonne yells at me when she thinks I have talked long enough, I shouted *stop talking* and turned away. But their quick departure haunted me. I started to wonder if maybe I had gone too far.

That night, I did a little research.

Apparently, there is an old Chinese custom that teaches girls to reject all compliments. To be objective, I did (for a whole long minute) *try* to tap into this tradition. But it was too big a shift for me. Setting girls up for failure is precisely the same in any culture.

Teach your students what they need to know, my first dance teacher said. I decided then and there that I wanted to become this kind of teacher. There is so much more to teach young dancers than technique and choreography.

It's my hope that my voice, and not the voice of criticism, will be the one this girl remembers whenever she hears something that makes her feel unworthy. If she thinks about my praise, and in so doing believes in herself a little more, my work is done. From wherever she stands, at the barre or in the world, I want her to feel confidence take hold. And that, as the years pass, she will know when it is being undermined, and find her way back to it in no time.

Dance was never meant to be a competition, no matter how many TV shows enforce the damaging idea that there always needs to be a winner and a loser, because there is more money in promoting the stage this way.

I want to teach dancers that it *is* possible to live their lives uncompetitively (other than with ourselves) even in the face of a culture that values sport over art, with a limited idea of what "success" is.

This is the voice that rose to the surface, the one that needs to say that "success" is a private dance with only two steps.

First, choose what makes you happy.

Secondly, go after it. No matter what anyone says.

Especially about your body.

I Should Have Listened

My father wants to know why so much of my writing fails to mention him. "You only write about your mother," he said.

"Not always," I say.

But you know how it is. After the divorce, it's one against the other. And there is no better way to please them than to give *their* qualities the advantage.

So, Dad? A few days back, just as the daffodils came into bloom, I did write about you. Remember when I fell head over heels in love with that 1950's cottage in Port Townsend, and you told me to have the pipes inspected before we bought it?

Well, I never told you, but a month after moving in, I was on my knees in the bathroom, crying because the city sewer backed up through the shower drain, something I didn't even know *could* happen. And not one part of me knew where to begin with the regret or the clean-up.

"Cedar roots dig their way into the pipes," the plumber said, and I felt regret for rushing into things, for buying a house faster than a swallow can swoop.

I tried to remember how, before buying the house, I'd walk out to the street and look back at it, and how it never failed to amaze me how much pleasure it gave me. It was a strange sensation, too, because I knew I was clueless about all-things-maintenance. But as soon as we moved in, I felt hugely connected to the present in my house from the past and that's the funny thing about contradiction, how we can embrace things emotionally even when our brains suspect otherwise.

The worst part was the stench. That's what really got me. The overflowing sickening odor distinctive to porta potties, septic tanks, and cesspools. Plus, there was heat coming through, mucky, manure-y, *heat*.

How does anyone even *face* such a mess? It wasn't like other messes. I couldn't just close the door so I wouldn't have to look at it until I was good and ready.

Let me remind you that I've never changed a poopy diaper in my life. As a kid, I'd babysit next door, sure, but I'd call up my mother the moment the baby started to smell and she'd rush over. (How did I get this far in life without remembering to thank her for that?)

I would have to sell the house, I reasoned. Or burn it down. I even thought about locking the bathroom door and digging an outhouse. It could work.

Where to begin?

Wearing rain boots and manned with a spatula, a serving spoon, and rolls and rolls of *Bounty*, I dove in.

This is the kind of task you undertake with whatever means you can find, and as soon as you begin you get this awful feeling of how terrible it is and how long it will take, but you stay in there swinging until the chore is complete. And in the hours it took to buff my bathroom back into any memory of the pride I once had for it, I kept thinking that were it possible to return my house like a dress that doesn't quite work once I get it home, I would have.

Dad, the thing is, you called in the middle of all this. And when I heard you ask me how it was going, I didn't pick up. I'm sorry.

I dragged three Hefty bags to the curb. I decided not to wash my boots, just to throw them in.

That night I kept listening for noises from the bathroom, but all was quiet. It took another few hours, but I was finally able to let go of buyer's remorse, or it finally let go of me, I'm not sure which, but either way, I slept.

But I wasn't able to turn my fiasco into an amusing story to share with you, Dad, handing it over with a plucky little laugh, until now. After I picked up a photo of the house, the one I keep on a shelf with other old friends, I knew it was time to come clean.

Dad, I was starry-eyed and impulsive.

And because I know what he really wants to hear, I make sure to say, "I should have listened to you. You were right."

I close my eyes and think about this man who gave me life. As a girl, I feared him, but I have come to think of him as the more fragile one, so I add, "You are *always* right."

Because if there is one thing life has taught me (despite all my so-called feminism), it's that if you want to make a fragile man happy, you hand over a little more reign, a little white lie, a little fib, a little fiction.

Whatever little it takes.

INNOCENCE

I LIKE TO TAKE WALKS. One step in front of another, as I work through the countless emotional complexities that come with being alive, until I am sure that tomorrow will be better than today.

Today I walk along North Beach. And you might not think that something as familiar as two girls laughing and splashing in the waves would be my greatest new reason to believe in a better day, but they are.

On a sandy shoreline, they are.

On a cloudy day in Seattle, they are.

I think, *girls, you are the reason I've come!*

Am I hoping to stare my way back to a time when my whole life seemed still yet to happen? When desires and possibilities dangled so near, it felt as if I could reach out and touch them?

Of course. But it also brings our opposite moods into stark focus—I laugh, too, but I don't *feel* like laughing.

I meant to leave my mood at home. I had the best intentions. But disappointment had already spread through me like kerosene inching up a wick. And the thing is, I can't even remember which disappointment it was.

It's always like this. Something good happens and I am filled with a sense of accomplishment. Then, just as suddenly, a setback—which, as you know, happens pretty regularly—and in no time defeat has its way with me again. Defeat positively *thrives*.

I don't mean to sound ungrateful. There are much worse fates than defeat. But my scope can sometimes shrink into something more limited, more stubborn; it won't grow. And it's hard with no coworkers to complain to. And you do *not* want to complain about being a writer to your friends who are waiting on tables for a living, or dealing with passive-aggressive teammates in Big Tech, or deferring to bossy real estate brokers, fussy kids and/or aging parents.

Besides, deep down, it's never one disappointment. It's the whole risk of putting yourself out there *now* while trying not to succumb to fears from before. Fears that are sure you said or did the wrong thing, convinced that you blew it, pointing a scolding finger at you at three o'clock in the morning. Watching the girls is a relief from all that.

Take note—innocence today is a specific way of layering one T-shirt over another. It is vivid tattoos. It is a way of speaking that can't help inserting the word "like" over and over like a tick. It's a preference for "no problem" over "you're welcome," as if kindness *could* be a problem, potentially. Until I end up shaking my head because there will never be another time in my life as distinctly innocent, not if I live to be a hundred and ten.

I turn my head at the sight of a middle-aged woman texting as she walks down the beach. Texting while walking has never made sense to me, but when she trips over driftwood and looks back with annoyance as if it's the log's fault, now *this* does make me laugh.

I turn back to the girls, to how the whole idea of closeness, our need for it, seems to come more naturally to them. Or maybe it just comes more naturally by the sea. I stay with this thought until my doubts are not (as) doubtful anymore. They run off. Wash away. After I read that amniotic fluid has the same salt composition as sea water, all my beliefs on why that would be settled into place. We begin in the sea. Far from the limitations of lake waters. And never mind those raging rivers that can only shoot us in one direction.

I sigh when it's time to go.

To the girls I whisper, *you are strong and smart and capable, and what I hope is that you will soon know how strong and smart and capable you are, because the world really needs strong, smart, capable women right about now.*

And with that, I actually bow my head.

Summer Dresses

Bottom line, I live for summer.

More to the point, summer *dresses*. I think dresses are art, that's all.

And a woman in Seattle can long for a chance to wear her favorites. By July, mine are just dying to get out. In fact, I've been known to change clothes three times a sunny day just to be sure I get to wear them all before the drizzle returns.

"So," I say to Larry, holding up a halter dress bordered with leaves near the neckline. "I am deeply in love with this one. I thought you should know."

This makes my good man smile. He knows to let me be my most Italian-self when warm weather strikes.

The dress and I found each other at the Nordstrom Rack. Sale dresses were marked down another fifty percent and women tutted in and out of the racks like chickens in search of food. When I spotted the dress, my heart beat a little faster and by the time the earth revolved once I'd already worn it twice.

But what I really love about the dress is that it makes me think of a-friend-I-will-not-name. She has a place in my thoughts today because two months ago she met a man.

And next week she will marry him!!

Yes, twin exclamation points. That's how worried I am.

We were on the ferry when she told me. She lowered her voice, looked port and starboard, as if the border patrol listened in. "Why are you whispering?" I said.

"It's just, well, I know you don't like him."

I tried to smile. "It's not like next time I see him, I'm going to . . ." at a loss for words, I quoted the familiar DHS warning from the poster above her head, "see something suspicious and say something."

"Promise?"

She was referring to what I said right after she told me they were seeing each other. I have always tried to be supportive of my friend's opinions, even if I can't keep from giving mine, and in this case, mine went something like, "Oh god no! No, no, no. You cannot trust him!"

Her wedding is the last weekend in August and I'm wearing a dress that is practically up to here, only because she dared me, and I agreed because I thought wearing a dress she picked out for me might smooth things over between us. I don't want her to think I disapprove of anything else, in any major way, any time soon.

"I'll fix you right up," she said, "it'll be fun."

It *was* fun. Whether it was the fact we'd come together for the sole purpose of coaxing me into one too-young-for-me dress after another, or the sound of our voices cracking jokes about my creased knees or hers, I can't say, but I would have worn a babushka if she'd asked me to.

Because it's her wedding.

Because, in her company, I've grown more comfortable exposing my epidermis.

Did I mention she is from Brazil? Shiny black ponytail, gold hoop earrings, gorgeous. No matter how exotically-Italian I fool myself into believing I am, I always feel a tad frumpy next to her. And when your most-fashionable friend isn't afraid to show a little skin, it casts a spell. Until I no longer want to dress Northwest Reserve. She gives my legs permission to show themselves.

After trying on everything in my closet even close to wedding-able, finally there was one dress that made me say, "I could maybe wear this." I had to hold my breath while she zipped me up and that effort alone totally restored us to not avoiding each other's eyes when she talked about *him*.

Once I had the dress on, I don't think anyone could have pried it off me. I wanted to prance around in the dress, jump up and down in the dress, dance to Michael Jackson's *The Way You Make Me Feel* in the dress.

Happily, I was not alone. She and I share a primal relationship to music. All women should have a friend they can dance with on a dime, simply drop what they are doing and *move*. I said, "When I think of all the times I said a woman our age has no business dressing this way."

"Well, you could wear Capri-chinos and those awful shoes that look like rodent cages, it's entirely up to you. Seriously, someone needs to ban Capri-chinos."

My friend doesn't like the way American women dress, doesn't believe women were meant to wear pants all the time, says that, from behind, you can't tell the women from the men. "Unimaginative" is one of her more gracious comments.

She also likes to remind me that because of my DNA, I have a duty to let my femininity flourish.

Our style is open, our friendship genuine.

Even if this new husband doesn't work out, she and I will make it through.

Seedling

I'VE NEVER QUITE GOTTEN OVER how good it feels to receive kudos from a reader.

Lydia-on-Capitol Hill, thank you. For the compliment and for the photo. Your blue highlights make you seem like a woman who knows how to push past comfort zones. I say this because if you don't think you had anything to do with the story I am about to tell, I want you to know that you had everything.

So, on the heels of your generosity, I want to say that keeping up with hairstyle trends does not really matter to me.

But they *do* matter to me.

Just not all that much.

Of course, to my hairdresser they matter a lot. She's been trying to get me to update my cut and color for years. Finally, one day after she said "really?" as if the word was a test, I gave in. I didn't quite understand the whole permanent vs. semi-permanent thing, so I was taking my time trying to grasp all of the advantages and disadvantages, and wrongly assumed she valued my thorough questioning.

Until she yawned.

Luckily, I am able to detect when I have digressed from *interested in the facts* to *unable to make a simple decision once I have them*. I apologized.

But I flat-out rejected her next suggestion, highlights. I even put my hand up to hold my ground. "Just what are you afraid of?" she said. Clearly a test, this time.

What, indeed. Because frankly, it wasn't the worst idea, and I knew it.

From there, I was tempted, then swayed, to remove the gray strands that run (or used to run) directly through my earlier and next selves, dissecting my self-image right down the middle. I'd been trying to accept them for some time. But even when a strong gust from the Gorge of Aging Gracefully blew on my ego with all of its might, I couldn't succumb. I hated the gray. I wanted it gone.

"And," she said after all the goop from her cup was gone, "you wouldn't want to let me do a cut because then you'd look ten years younger and no one wants *that*."

Pure manipulation. It purely worked. An hour later, my new haircut felt like, dare I say, *a gift from heaven*. Only the gift didn't stop with the hair on my head.

A woman smiled at me from a side doorway. Minutes later, I lay on a cot trying to think about anything else, like how her name tag said KATHY, and why don't they give Americans more credit for being able to remember names like *Quyen*, until she slapped my thigh and said, "it hurt a liddle, k?" struggling to suppress her amusement because, to my horror, notions of a bikini wax not hurting is wishful thinking. It's excruciating.

But it was nearly time for my return to Oahu. And though pubes poking their way out of a one-piece in the Northwest is acceptable, in Hawaii, pubes just won't do. The whole point of a bikini is to make you look. A friend who lives on the island said she can pick out the women vacationing from Washington and Oregon just by scanning the sand. "They wear one-pieces!" she said, as if they were breaking the law. The whole subject of bikinis came up when I told her about my wax. "But after weeks of sitting on the beach with nearly-naked women from all over the world," she explained, "they eventually go to Ala Moana and spend the afternoon trying on two-pieces."

"I long ago discarded any notion of looking good in a two-piece," I said.

"Mark my words, your two-piece will blossom into a bikini, and that will be your Lady Gaga moment."

"You'll have to fill me in on what that means," I said.

So, she started to sing to me: *I'm beautiful in my way 'Cause God makes no mistakes. I'm on the right track baby, I was born this way.*

The very next day I made my way to Macy's to get a head start on the process.

And did I judge myself harshly in the mirror?

No. I did not.

And did I buy the bikini?

Yes.

And highlights? Did I give in to the highlights?

Yes, Lydia, I did.

I am so highlighted, in fact, there is something vastly different about my appearance, but I am hard-pressed to tell you exactly *what* that something is. But it stirs a mild encouraging feeling within the pit of my stomach.

And I love that feeling. I always have.

The Taste of a Word

I have learned a lot about myself by looking back at a few previous writings about food.

Like my difficulty with turning it out in edible fashion.

But I want to be good at cooking. Good enough to have people over to dinner without stressing about it.

Good enough to be able to make something from scratch that looks appetizing.

"I don't know how you can eat like that," my mother said once, alluding to the can opener in my hand.

Listen, I'm fine with opening a can of garbanzo beans and pouring them over pre-washed salad. And I'm not just making light, my meals are uncomplicated. Likely because my work is exactly the opposite.

But that's only one reason.

Another is that early on, kids become aware of what their parents expect of them and choose to either fulfill those expectations or shrug them off. I'm afraid that with most things related to cooking, I chose the latter.

It's funny how choices can, and will, skip a generation.

Being the daughter of an Italian woman who dedicated her life to food in all its textures, types, and tweakings, my choice caused a frown that held everything she was thinking but wouldn't say. We became a mother who lives for cooking and a daughter who doesn't own a spatula, a garlic press, or, as she was quick to point out, "a decent set of pans for God's sake!"

"I'm sorry." I fibbed.

"I can't even find a measuring cup!" She was rooting around in my cupboard with an exasperated look on her face.

So, you can imagine how unfair I thought she was when, one Thanksgiving, she suggested *I* make the Tiramisu.

That is the word she used, "suggest." But we both knew she was ordering me to make it. She worried that I would never take her recipes to heart.

"Now, mom, I do love the *word* Tiramisu." I said, letting it flow off my tongue in the smoothest of syllables. "But I don't think I can pull off *making* it."

My mother hardly cared about my love of the word. She wanted only that I follow her instructions scribbled in the margins of an index card: *Not too much coffee! Sponge will turn soggy.*

Nor did she care about my *research*.

Such as: Tiramisu was created in Siena, Italy, in honor of a Grand Duke. *Zuppa del duca.* "Duke's soup," I said. "Introduced to America in San Francisco."

"You're not writing a book report," she said solemnly.

For weeks, the knowledge that I was to make the desert forced me to do what I'd probably always wanted to do, but was afraid to, which was to at least *try* to place something on our holiday table that I was proud of.

Because once upon a time that seems like yesterday, my mother was capable of making the entire Thanksgiving feast without asking for help from her career-obsessed daughter. I know this because I sat at her table and gorged myself year after year. And all I ever contributed is a bottle of Valpolicella and another story about how terrifying it is to imagine myself ever staging such a meal.

By the way, Tiramisu was served at my wedding when I, so young and aglow, knew nothing about anything except that my nuptial dessert would not be a three-layer-round gloating from the center of the table.

I think, subconsciously, I knew that learning to make Tiramisu would become another way of defining myself. And that to turn away from the responsibility would be like turning away from part of who I am.

On one level, anyway.

On another, I still don't take it all *that* seriously.

Another little insight into the effect a word can have—since the mere thought of moist, cocoa-y perfection can pick me right up—is that Tiramisu literally *means* "pick me up." And if there's one thing I know about everything either worthy or draining of my time, is that one appreciable remark from an editor, a reader, or even a total stranger is all it takes to turn a lousy day around.

Also significant to note—and why my mother emailed me her recipe with the important steps in **BOLD** block letters, <u>UNDERLINED,</u> UPPERCASE—is that the only other time I tried to make Tiramisu, well, my best guess at what went wrong is that I did, in fact, need to whisk the eggs until "stiff peaks" formed and **GENTLY** add them to the sugar before adding both **GRADUALLY** to the mascarpone. Rather than letting the eggs slide en masse from their shells directly into a bowl of Ladyfingers.

It's never wise to rush a delicate thing.

There would be no pulling a fast one this time. For my mother's last Thanksgiving, (as it turned out), I would need to **GET IT RIGHT**.

In one of my tiny notebooks, the kind writers carry because there is no such thing as a reliable memory, I wrote down something I heard a chef say years ago at a cooking demonstration, where I'd wedged my way into the crowd for the free food and wound up staying because the chef was smart, funny, and clearly loved the fact he'd captivated a throng of smiling women. He was burly, too, like he could comfortably pick any one of us up under one arm and continue whisking with the other. "Some foods are delicious lies that make us believe in heaven," he said, before popping a slice of espresso-soaked Tiramisu into his mouth.

Everyone clapped with pleasure.

Why I wrote down such a corny saying, I have no idea. I suppose I thought it *meant* something.

Turns out, it did.

Bonnie

I struggle with December.

As the month approaches, my interest in it retreats.

It's the over-sentimentality of the season, I tell myself, until I remember my first real friend. From third grade through high school, we were inseparable.

Naturally, we moved on. For a decade we hung on as best we could. Out in the world without anyone who knew us before, at least we still had each other.

As the years passed, I thought about her less, but whenever we did speak, I worried more. But as long as the therapist was helping, and she swore she was, I felt like she would ultimately rise out of her depression, that it wouldn't do her in. Her long history of physical, alcohol, and drug abuse was not exactly a recipe for success, but there she was, still trying to put the worst behind her. I thought that if anyone could outrun her past and endure whatever the future held in store for her, it was Bonnie.

At the time, I'm not sure I grasped how much the word "depressed," spoken by someone you love makes you afraid. I took her sadness to heart, that's what began to happen whenever I was with her, and I wasn't able to share this with her in a way that would make her feel less sad, that much I did grasp. Instead, I moved away from our friendship. Slowly at first, and then, though it pains me to say this now, making a beeline.

As Bonnie grew increasingly afraid of failure, of *life*, while I, on the other hand, wanted to seize the world with youthful enthusiasm, well, I couldn't, *wouldn't,* let myself carry the weight of her depression.

I felt stifled by it.

Instead, I sought out friends who were more like the person I wanted to become: lighter, confidant, creative.

This is only clear to me now, of course, in hindsight.

When I received the call, twelve years ago, on December 2nd, that Bonne had taken her own life, I stood staring out the window at everything about my neighborhood that seemed the same: Space Needle glowing, Christmas lights twinkling. This is the cruelest part about losing someone, how the world powers on while you crumble inside. And I started thinking all kinds of selfish thoughts about myself.

That was what the next few months were all about: *guilt.*

It was then that I came to believe that doing something as simple as tending a garden can offset things like guilt. I was relieved by any act of responsibility. My balcony got a lot of attention that year. I potted and repotted until I realized—or part of me realized—that her depression had nothing to do with me. That my yearning to thrive, to be a writer, a dancer, *myself,* was the only way *I* could survive. And I needed to do so with as many positive, productive people as I could find along the way.

My stability depended on balancing everyday life with extraordinary goals.

It still does.

So here I am, finally, able to admit that Bonnie felt like too much ballast for someone hoping to soar. So, I cut her off.

At her service, friends did what friends do, leaving flowers and food and saying usual things like, "she can finally rest in peace," while my first thought was how could anyone rest peacefully after what she'd been through?

But now?

I steal courage from the words. They free me (temporarily) from the nagging truth: *I abandoned her.* So, I cling to them.

We cling to all kinds of clichés when we are desperate.

Though, lately, I'm more inclined to say, *Rest, my friend, in peaceful silence. And forgive me, forgive me please, for suggesting you carry on with your life while I carry on with mine.*

Many emotions still have their way with me come December, but I haven't faulted myself (not as often, anyway) for needing to find my way into a life that made sense to me, even if it meant leaving a friend behind with a disease that did not.

Today, I'm less interested in blaming myself for all kinds of single-minded things I needed to do in order to get *here*, where I am still determined to throw open the curtains and feel the light on my face.

Even on the darkest days.

But with more compassion for those who cannot.

And though my compassion still has smidgins of regret layered into it, I no longer try to remove them. I just let myself fall down into that sorry layer for a while.

A few hours at most.

It's not any fun. It's very fatiguing.

But it feels deeply loyal to Bonnie.

Because maybe she is still counting on me. Who knows?

Yet Again

I DON'T KNOW HOW MUCH LONGER I can live in a condo. Seriously.

I'm looking at houses again.

And there is one I am a little taken with. (I know. I know.)

I keep parking out front.

Sometimes I park a block away so that I can stroll up to it more slowly, view it as a stranger would. If I walk closer, I might even see a woman in her garden and think, *I don't have time for such a big garden, I am nothing like you.*

Except at the moment, I am.

Or I want to be.

By my third visit, I've read all the information I could find at the library about affordable restoration of an older house, one that is considered a little shabby, even kitschy by some of its neighbors who live in basically the same tan or white ranch.

In such reserved company, an original must prevail on her own, head held high.

I know this.

Not to say the house isn't admired, she is, just not readily accepted as a "local."

Whatever that word even means in a city of transplants my friend Jeff said suffers from Stockholm Syndrome. When I asked him what he meant by that he said, "We are slowly taking on the characteristics of our geeky captors. But here's the thing, I *want* to talk to someone when I buy groceries. I *like* driving my own car."

Yesterday I told my librarian, "My husband is trying to talk me out of the house."

"That's because he's a sensible man," she said.

She gives me good insight along with my books, so it hardly matters *when* I came to trust her. What matters is that I *do*.

Our conversations began years ago in a low register at the counter. The friendship we've developed since has never gone beyond the walls of the Carnegie, but it is continually a lesson in how much easier it is to be yourself when you don't feel yourself trying; how much better we get at being ourselves in certain company.

I have her to thank for that.

My fondest memory of her was the day I overheard her tell a particularly ornery man who spends his afternoons in the library to stop pestering unsuspecting walk-ins with his political views. Obama had just sent more troops into Afghanistan and tempers were flaring even at the library. "Old age," she said in a loud whisper, "is not an excuse to be disrespectful." To chance upon my librarian admonishing a man so tactfully was like seeing a bud open.

I am always struck by the sheer sight of her as she speeds through the aisles, stops, selects a title, hurries back to the front desk in brisk strides, two steps for every one of mine.

She always gets to the point so much faster than I do.

She is so perceptive.

Even about houses, I soon came to realize.

A Week Later

I'd been so busy talking up the house's second-floor balcony, I hadn't considered the fact that it was supported by wood beams that had, according to my husband, already turned to compost.

"You mean the whole thing could cave in?" I said, nervously.

He looked at me as if to say, *it has already caved in.*

I stuck my finger into the mushy-soft wood and happily trotted behind him back to the car.

A Month Later

"When you find the right house, you'll know, my friend Lynette said.

"How will I know? Will it say my name over the door?"

"Something like that," she laughed. "But first you'll likely get a really good feel for what you *don't* want."

"And if I don't know exactly what I don't want?"

I said that. But I remember feeling as though I knew exactly what I didn't want, and what I did, and that it would be easier to find this time, surrounded by flowering shrubs.

And so, it all begins wonderfully again. I feel tingles.

Until, well, was Lynette ever right.

There are cracks in the foundation. Something has to give.

And hidden obstacles. Like mold behind the wallpaper.

And obvious ones like peeling linoleum floors, avocado appliances (the old avocado), rugs that smell of cigarette smoke, bathrooms that smell like kitty litter, noisy neighbors because I can *hear* them.

There are front steps you can fall through if you don't hang on to the railing you can fall through if you don't hang on to your realtor who is about to topple off her wedge-heel ankle boots.

There are rickety porch slats and vines so thick I can hear my husband yelling, "Ivy works like a ratchet until the whole thing collapses!"

I make notes.

My realtor suggests another place and off we go as she chirps on about vinyl siding and who-knows-what-all, and I say things like "French doors would be nice," and she politely points out (again) that my expectations exceed my finances. Until it all becomes more about places I can afford. And what fun is that?

I should have known better than to believe we were headed in the right direction because suddenly we were on the freeway bypassing everything I love about Seattle and headed north, way north, suburban north, North*gate*.

"Are you trying to humor me?" I said.

The last straw was when we drove right up to yet another yellow, green, and orange "revitalization" condo on Pill Hill, an intersection where two major hospitals come together in several medically detached blocks off Madison, and I was shaking my head before we even got out of the car. She looked at me. And I can safely say that what I saw in her eyes were these very words: *This* is where a woman of your age and means belongs.

And it occurs to me to take another break from home-hunting altogether. This feels right to me. Because I may never find *the* house, and I want to stop looking before my desire turns into despair.

Which is where desire often heads when the pressure mounts.

By Heart

Trying to find the words to describe how it feels to be the friend of an alcoholic, well, I'm not sure I have managed it all that well. The friendship, or this narrative.

The sky is darkening fast, earlier and earlier now, as if remembering the last time my friend and I talked on the phone isn't enough to make me feel gloomy.

We were having one of our snappy little debates about the Ferris Wheel by the ferry landing. She thought it made the waterfront feel more inviting. And "safer."

Except the word came out as "thafer."

I insisted a Ferris Wheel is more about imitating other cities than representing ours, sounding more troubled than I intended because my friend was getting drunk at two in the afternoon. On a weekday. I could hear her taking sips.

Realistically, I know no one can stop another from drinking, but a challenge, a *dare*, if you will, urged me to own up to my fear of, and imperfect knack for, the head-banging, risky work friendship can be sometimes, if you can stomach it. Versus my need to do the work all the same.

We all have our issues.

But in the world we are living in, increasingly distant and remote, where conversations we need to have are constantly usurped by technology, I feel it's even more important to talk.

So, when I asked if she was maybe drinking a little too much again, and she said, "I am just so *over* Seattle," I feared that she was really saying she was just so over *me*. She is about to move to Los Angeles and major life changes can necessitate a bit of I'm-so-over-you. Which she was demonstrating. Rather blatantly.

Sometimes people just want to start over, wipe the slate clean.

I was already trying to fill in the miles about to separate us by talking about the Ferris Wheel in the first place. Because I couldn't ask *the* question. The question that stresses what I keep failing to understand: that key to the way an alcoholic views the world is by *escaping* it.

Also. Isn't Los Angeles the last place on earth an alcoholic (who is always mentioning how lonely she feels) should move to?

As soon as I hung up, I knew that I'd have to find a way to go about proving I wasn't afraid to be honest anymore, beginning with my friendships. Because for women, after the men disappear for whatever reasons—unfaithfulness, without saying why, death, because we *want* them out—friendship may be our next, and for some, our only, love life left. And if we screw it up, ultimately, the fallout is not the same as a divorce. It can feel even worse. My own mother said as much.

But knowing I want to be better at something doesn't help me figure out how to bring up a hard truth while making it soft enough for two grown women to land on. I can't fly off the handle. Or hold it in too long, that's the worst thing for any relationship. It has to unfold carefully. Knowingly. The way a parachute unfurls. Otherwise, we will be one person looking contemptuously at another.

And the only way to learn how to do this is . . . honestly? I haven't a clue.

By "heart" is all that comes to me. I will need to muddle through with heart.

More heart.

Rich expanses of heart.

No Can

To WRITE ABOUT ANYONE but him, my mother's last *aloha* (the Hawaiian word for love) would be impossible today.

Just impossible.

And even if this kind of directive bothers me, I would never ignore it.

It's a long story as to how my mom ended up on Oahu. But there's a shorter version: Her second husband was a Ukulele player, and in the years they were married, I flew to the island dozens of times.

In the beginning, the skies opened to the fullest blue imaginable. But with time, as soon as I stepped from the plane, they began to close in.

What I mean is, nothing prepares you for the natural order of things. I stood at the foot of my mother's bed feeling as if the cord that held me to earth was slipping away. The worst part was I had to be present, or try to be, without letting my mind fall back into all the memories, good and bad. Because this is what the mind does, it thinks and thinks and thinks. It won't let up.

Which can make you look older by years. One TSA agent sat up to look at my license and back to my face three times. I saw her uncertainty.

I *felt* her uncertainty.

I think what troubled her most was that someone could look so tired and still be standing. When she finally handed my license back, we both did our best to smile.

After finally clicking my seat belt, I must have sighed louder than I thought.

"I know," my seatmate grumbled, "I would never come back here, either."

What? I could understand a critical remark or two aimed at Waikiki. A lot of us find out the hard way how disappointing it can be. We think we are about to visit a "tropical paradise" and what we find is an overpriced shopping strip and a receding beach.

But the entire island is not like this and I wondered if she'd bothered to find that out. My first drive around the perimeter enlightened me to the grace much of Oahu still is. Provided, of course, you ignore the fact that most of it is slated for development of one kind or another. As well as the military factor, the rail debacle, and too many tourists.

Speaking of, my seatmate started to *tsk* her tongue at all the sunburned travelers making their way down the aisle. And when you need peace, you do not want to sit next to someone making that awful *tsk-tsk* sound, muttering out the side of their mouth about everything they find amiss. "Homeless people on the beach? I can walk to Pioneer Square if I want homeless, *tsk-tsk.*"

I came this close, *this* close, to saying, "Please shut up. There are good people here."

I was thinking of the Hospice nurses and volunteers in Palolo Valley, living angels in my book. "There are things daughters are not meant to hear," one said to me after offering to sit and talk to my mom every day until I could sew up loose ends at home and return. I was leaving my mother with a woman close to her own age with real knowledge to share, and when guilt got the best of me she said, "You've found the guts to find your own purpose. Your mother is so proud of you."

I felt such a sharp stab of want for my mother who was not really there to be my mother anymore, so the mothering I received from this kind stranger made me see that we may not always get the mothering we need when we need it the most and that is when any wise mothering will do.

I thought of one nurse in particular, my mother's beloved (as right up to the end she loved to flirt), a mild man of local mix: part Filipino, part Haole, part Chinese. A gentle soul.

Gentle souls are hard to find.

I can still picture him placing a single Plumeria behind my mother's ear until she, sensing his touch, would stare up at him with such affection in her eyes. I asked myself what he would say to the awful woman seated next to me. His answer didn't hesitate. "Eh! Don't talk stink about our island. No can!"

I never thought of myself as a mean seatmate, but I told the woman that I didn't want to listen to her. Then. Ever.

As soon as the words left my mouth, I felt like I finally understood what my mother meant, and the satisfied smile on her face when she said it, all those years ago when she slammed down the phone on Mrs. McKenzie—our next-door neighbor who complained often about everything, you name it—that sometimes you just need to dismiss someone because they don't *deserve* you. "Every time I talk to that woman, she kills a little part of my soul," my mother said, sweeping her hands over the sides of her bosom, distinctly Italian somehow.

So there you have it, a little story about the kind of person who can ruin your day.

And another about those who offer so much aloha, they manage to save it.

LET ME SPEAK

IT'S BEEN AN INTERESTING WEEK.

On Monday, I was overcome by the downsides of public speaking and it took me until Friday to understand *why*.

It all began at the Bellevue Club where I felt behind, fashion-wise, nowhere near Eastside enough, but that wasn't the troubling part. I just didn't feel like the men and women were behind me, possibly due to the steady stream of texts I was competing with. At one point, I imagined fighting off the pings with flailing arms. *Please, just let me speak and I'm out of here*!

Social behavior can take a toll lately. If I am not able to rise above the distraction, I cannot give anything near my best, and I'm afraid that's what happened.

That is putting it mildly. I bombed.

What I mean is . . . it was an evening I would rather forget. But I can't. And I worry they won't forget either.

I've always been a bit of a disappointment to myself on the Eastside. It's just too *some*thing over there. Too new, too moneyed, too corporate. It shuts me down inside.

One saying got me through that talk: *Resilience grows one try at a time.*

The next day my audience was in Port Townsend. To put things in their simplest terms, Port Townsend is about as far away from Bellevue, mentally, as one can drive in a day. I used to live in Port Townsend, so I was essentially speaking in front of family. This takes guts, let me tell you. Family asks a lot of you. But I never lost my confidence. They were so behind me, I naturally wanted to give more of myself.

The next evening, I addressed the North Olympic Land Trust Harvest Dinner where, as soon as I arrived, I was swept up in nostalgia for the life I used to live in Sequim. I sipped a lovely glass of wine while catching up with my old friend, R.

Which sounds fun and all, but my golden rule is that I never drink anything before addressing an audience. But when you return to your past, you are bound to forget a few of your present responsibilities.

Consequently, I don't have a clear memory of how well I did that night. I got through it okay, but all I remember is how hard I had to focus to stay on book because alcohol can make me say things a little too true. Without apology.

Seeing my old friend again reminded me how, at the onset of my career, I sought such a highly accomplished writer as a friend because I liked getting to know the writer I thought I was becoming. But as time flew by (and to most writers this means more rejections than we care to count), I purposely made friends with younger people who weren't writers, thank god, who seemed to keep things fresh, livelier, less competitive.

Or so I told myself.

What was really happening was fear pressed down tremendously hard, demanding I compete at a level that made me feel like I couldn't keep up. Time away from my desk felt costly. I felt caught in a web of expectation and it wore me out. I stopped calling R.

In a sense, my younger friends gave me a breather from the pecking order, allowed me to feel more prolific, ahead of the game, and reminded me not to fear the challenges ahead but to count myself lucky for having them to fear at all.

Basically, they cut me a break.

But something happened when my back was turned. Instead of offering a reprieve, they began to remind me how quickly time was slipping past. And I wasn't ready for this feeling yet, this queasiness in my stomach where insecurity settles. I understood what a risk it was to reach out to R. again, but reach out I did.

Naturally, she too had moved on. Leaving me with no other close writer friend.

Though it pains me to say this now, because as soon as I saw her again, she said, "I've missed you!" I can't imagine why I ever thought such crazy competitive thoughts in the first place.

But it's a crazy competitive ride if you want to get anywhere as a writer. (I even considered murder once. Well, not *murder,* exactly, as in killing someone, but after he said what he said and did what he did, I thought about sending a career-killing email. Oh, the betrayal I felt!)

I had no understanding that my new awareness of time passing that drove me in those years—so strong it felt like a tide ebbing, the way you feel when your feet sink in wet sand—is why I began to work as though writing was a contest, a *race*.

Experience has taught me to slow down, to work at a more satisfying pace.

But at the time, I kept on racing until, on the positive side, I found the nerve to start asking for the kind of money I deserve to speak in front of one audience after another. I just had to find the muscle (and the ability to ask for what we want *is* a muscle) to train myself that accepting less is not my due.

And for a near-year after, a year I believed would change everything (it didn't), I felt as if, finally, I had achieved *enough*. I was more accepting of how much time it takes to realize our dreams. I was full of new energy for my work. I was lifted out of strive-fatigue. I was enjoying the ride again.

And it's funny, but today my confidence has absolutely nothing to do with how much money I am paid. I'm grateful for this full circle, this turn of events.

Especially after R. let slip what she is paid to speak.

No wonder I reached for the wine.

I believe I reached into my gut for a swig of resilience, too.

Just to be on the safe side.

Magic

Before I moved to Seattle, I had never spent time thinking about when summer begins. If someone had asked me, I would have said, "In June. Or as early as May."

But a Northwest summer—the way people do not seem to mind wearing hats and gloves on the fourth of July—was a surprise I had to get used to.

But this all changes on a day like today, long-awaited, wonderfully warm. I may even take a dip in the sea. A *plunge*.

But first I promised to drive North to my friend Beth's place.

Beth sprained her ankle. Recently divorced, she's had no choice but to let her grass grow wild. And while friends are trying to help her through the "crisis months" (her words), no one volunteered to mow her lawn after her neighbor suggested that she do so with a little more frequency, please, so *I* volunteered.

As soon as I pull into her driveway, I can see how he obsesses about his lawn, her neighbor does. It is weed free, smooth as a putting surface, and mowed to within an inch of its life.

I like Beth's yard so much better. We are women who are never going to care about perfect lawns. "So I'll be mowing the dandelion's then?" I asked.

"That's about it," she said. "Or the putz next door is going to have a heart attack."

Beth isn't one for holding back.

Rolling out the mower made me remember another lawn-obsessive.

At the age of twenty-eight, I moved onto my own plot of land in Port Townsend where my neighbor rushed over to tell me in a slightly perturbed voice that every one of my dandelions has hundreds of seeds. To which I answered, "They also make great salads." She stood there for a minute and then she stomped off.

Fine by me.

The second time, she handed me a spray bottle of Round-Up without the slightest embarrassment, which I handed right back, also without embarrassment, after informing her that Round-Up is an herbicide defoliant. "Agent Orange in different packaging, basically," I said. "It kills every insect and worm in the soil, consequently killing the birds who eat them, and according to the World Health Organization is apparently killing us, too. I'm sure you've read *Silent Spring*?"

I knew how far back I was reaching. But that book's warning will always be the great white shark of my childhood, circling close.

Then she did something that really pleased me, she left my yard and never came back.

Beth reads my column, so I'll have to tell her what I'm about to say, that whenever I drive into her development (there are gates), my suburbia-anxiety rises a notch. It's like there is not enough air, enough circulation; all the magic is gone.

Nor can I help comparing my neighborhood, where if I pluck a handful of leaves and chuck them to the sidewalk, I never worry what the neighbors will say. Foliage is an acceptable form of littering where I live. Partly because city maintenance blows the sidewalks clean once a week, building maintenance blows it once a *day*, and partly because I have lost every leaf-blower argument I have ever found myself in, consequently losing my first, second, and final round with the condo board who unanimously sided with maintenance status-quo, rather than my suggestion that the crew use a good old rake and broom.

No?

An electric blower, then? To cut the noise level.

No, again.

So I reason that if I'm forced to listen to a modern penchant for powerful, earsplitting machinery to blow away weightless flora, I will take full advantage and use the street as my compost bin.

But mostly I get away with it because no one cares. No one is about to walk up and tell me that my handful of leaves conflicts with their idea of picture-perfect.

It's a relief, anonymity. Especially after driving out to Beth's.

I bend down to fire up the mower. It starts on the first pull. How much fun it is to blow the first gush onto the putz's lawn. Out of the corner of my eye I see him yanking on a pair of work gloves. Beth laughs so hard she has to go inside.

Why would I not take advantage of a chance to make Beth laugh at a time like this?

"You never want to think of one of your neighbors as a total prick, but that's what he is," she said before I left.

Bored maybe, but I don't think he is a total prick. I do think he is a scapegoat, though.

I think Beth is just so angry at her ex.

Angry as soon as she wakes. Angry before turning in.

And the scapegoat, well, he is, at least, keeping her laughter alive.

And while driving away, I begin to sense the bigger picture: *laughter* is the magic. Wherever you can find it, wherever you live.

This thought cheered me up so much that I was able to drive through the exit gate without the slightest anxiety.

The bigger picture is my survival tool. It catches the light. That's the perfect metaphor. *It cuts through the dark.*

Natural Ease

It's a lost state I find myself in.

I don't really know how to fill the hours.

I am staring out the window, wondering who else is eyeing the Space Needle.

My friend Steph said I look relaxed, but the outside of someone is often so different from their inside.

As gratifying as my recent book launch was, it still stands out as one of the most bewildering times in my life. All through the weeks, the realization that once it was over, the whole process would need to begin again, well, I think most writers can relate when I say it's hard to enjoy the between time when the question *what's next?* is already knocking at the door.

To ease myself, I decide to meet my friend Seth for coffee, something I seldom do. He loves to go out for coffee, but it isn't like this for me. I think about it, but the part of me who prefers mornings at home in her sweats generally wins out.

But Seth is someone I can talk to, be myself with, so with two creamy caffeinated equivalents of dessert, we head down to the Water Taxi that will whisk us over to Alki.

I believe there are everyday events that we sense are going to help us even if we don't know how. Or why. Just that they will.

This is what happens when I spot the little girl wearing a hijab—hair, neck, and shoulders covered—sitting crossed-legged with her family (men, women, numerous children) on a huge woven mat under a clear plastic tarp secured by halved Clorox bottles filled with sand. Between them, a feast is spread in large tin foil containers. The food smells so good, Seth and I spend a long moment inhaling its tang. "Do you think they could be our new best friends?" Seth says.

It occurs to me that there are scores of twenty/thirty-somethings moving to my neighborhood from all over the world to work at Amazon, yet I rarely see an entire family together.

When I say as much to Seth, he changes the subject. Not dismissively, it's just that one mention of the word "Amazon" can send him into a tailspin. "Doesn't it strike you as a con to see Bezos's empire rise from the depths of Sixth Avenue after he convinced the world that no one needs a brick and mortar presence anymore, and now he *is* the biggest brick and mortar presence?"

Seth's insights are some of my favorite grasps of how the economy works. Like my trusty flat iron, I rely on him to set things straight.

"Sorry," he said, and quickly returned to what I'd said about families. "Immigrant families tend to live south of the economic wall that divides Seattle. Take the light rail to the airport if you don't believe me."

"It's always the same," I say. "The high cost of living defines what neighborhood we live in."

"I think it's more about ethnicity."

He's right. Growing up on the East Coast taught me the importance of the word. How people want to live around their own no matter how much we throw the word *integration* around. Even so, I find the division troubling. Seattle is supposed to be better than this. We can't keep dividing up the world. It's all one big mess.

Under the tarp, the men throw arms around each other easily and often. Everyone is singing. The girl and her mother eat something I don't recognize, expertly with their hands. *What language are they speaking?* I wonder. *Have they found their way here from Africa by way of Europe?* I'm staring now. When one of the men smiles, I quickly turn my head away.

I look around the beach. Most people sit separately staring at their phones. No one is singing, not much laughter. Even the volleyball game is intense.

After a while, we gather up our things. Before we turn to go, I see that the girl's head scarf has fallen to her shoulders. When she shakes her hair free, the natural ease of her motion touches me. *You are bending the rules,* I think. *Good for you.*

All morning I'd been waiting to notice something or someone to remind me of how much bigger the world is than my troubles. How pointless it is to worry.

I am really glad to see your hair, your whole face, your fearlessness.

I just needed to get out of my office, stop thinking.

I think best when I am not thinking.

WAHOOSH

I WOULD HAVE SWORN when I was younger that I'd never imagine myself saying, "I don't want to travel again for a long, long time."

The story I told myself then was that I wanted to travel forever.

But I *have* been traveling, one city after another, for months. Master Classes they are called, where every level of my experience is engaged. Add to this getting to visit towns, cities, and countries I might not get to see otherwise, and I remind myself every day that it's one of the most satisfying things in life, to have work one loves.

But even in love, there is a lot of comparing that goes on.

I don't mean I compare my class to anyone else's. I'm way past competing with anyone but myself (pretty much) always.

I am referring to comparisons of another nature.

In fact, comparing is pretty much all I do for the first day or so. I'm intrigued as much by huge white farmhouses outside of Wenatchee as I am by turquoise and yellow cottages on Providenciales.

More houses create more contrasts that create more comparisons.

Until I start to compare the life in front of me to the one I left behind with all the doors and windows locked, full of my "stuff," both figuratively and real, in various stages of completion.

This is good, I tell myself. It's all part of the traveling cycle, the complex set of questions that assess the choices we have made.

Actually, I drive myself a little crazy with all the comparing that goes on as I imagine myself living one life after another after another.

Not to worry.

As the days pass, I realize that there are wonderful houses, hideous houses, excellent restaurants, terrible restaurants, stingy people, and generous people wherever I go.

It all happens so fast (in hindsight) and then the tedious airport again before I pull up to my home where, now wait just a minute, doesn't it look amazing?

And that's when familiarity connects me. To me. To the life I've worked so hard for.

At some point, the refrigerator door will close behind me, and there it is, the sound I know so well, the sound only *my* refrigerator makes. I open the door and let it close, *wahoosh,* just to hear it again.

And look at my Juliette balcony. How perfect is *that* for a dancer? I walk outside under the misty moonlight that fills *my* sky, the breeze that shakes the petals off *my* potted plants, and I think *my* life is so good.

Even if that sounds too schmaltzy or whatever.

And I doubt, I seriously doubt, that I can pull off going to Asia to teach for a month. Even if it pays so well. Because money can never top the kind of connection with everything I love about home, can it?

Even money that is, um, let me do the math . . . close to ten times what I'd make teaching in the States in a year.

A year!

I wrote this piece back in July.

By mid-August, my travel bag was packed.

The students were great, the students are always great.

The air quality, not so much. I laid awake for hours, lonely, with no view of sky, watching the grit amass against the windows, thinking how one breath can make all the difference between living and dying.

I don't want to travel again for a long, long time.

ALL I CAN DO

A FEW WEEKS BACK, I was asked by the facilitator of a retreat center to talk about "connecting to one's true path, living one's passion, that sort of thing."

I thought it would be fairly painless to share my thoughts on "that sort of thing." And that passion-seekers sounded like a particularly receptive audience. There are many reasons to attend a retreat, but it seemed to me that the women who would attend this one would be ones who do not feel like they are living their passion.

Or not living it enough.

Maybe they haven't quite found what their passion is. Or they don't know how to give themselves permission to find it, let alone live it.

But no matter where they stand on the matter, passion is a touchy subject. And it's no easy thing to decide whether I am going to say exactly how I feel about touchy matters without crossing a line (and lines are not always clear until it's too late) or wimp out and deal with the topic more cautiously, figure out whether the former or latter is the one my audience will respond to seeing as how they are mature women already, about as passionate as they can stand to be. Thank you very much.

But any sort of pandering is difficult for me.

It just is.

In fact, I'm often guilty of bringing too much honesty to a conversation. But once I do, I try not to apologize for it, which is no easy thing either, but I'm (slowly) getting better at it. I've spent so much energy apologizing when another choice of words, or a simple nod of the head, is really all I needed. It's taken me years to get over the idea that it's my job to nail every single appearance. It's my job to do the best I can under the existing circumstances, and that's about it.

That is all I can do.

And it is a good thing I have come to this conclusion. Because, as it turns out, passion-seekers can be tough nuts to crack open. Though I don't want to get into that.

Well, yes, I do.

All I can figure is that they've spent so many years in a holding pattern, not making the genuine connections they now crave, so they are tongue-tied. Or they blather on and on, eager to hear themselves talk. Which is not making a connection either.

When I finished my talk, I sat next to a woman who clapped for me with her arms way up over her head, so I thought she'd be easy to talk to. Receptive, at least.

How wrong I was. I couldn't get her to open up about one personal thing. It was so disappointing. I kept thinking, *give me something other than a rundown of your children's lives. I'm meeting YOU. I want to hear about YOU.*

I kept up my end of the chitchat right through to the frosted cake slice, and finally excused myself, wanting nothing more than to get home to a hot bath.

I understand that not everyone will agree with me about the amount of intimacy one should, or even hope to, expect from social conversation. But there are many traits to my character I'm not especially proud of, and impatience is one of them. And in situations like this, I've grown hopelessly impatient. I just don't feel like I have the time to try to get to know someone who doesn't want to be, or doesn't know *how* to be, known.

As soon as I was safely inside the nearest bathroom stall, I wrote this down: ADD TO TALK: Try, please try, to reveal something truthful about ourselves—doubts, insecurities, fears, what makes us feel most alive, or disappoints us. WILLINGNESS is the definition of a passionate person.

The next day I gave a talk at The Rainier Club on Fourth Avenue downtown. The air inside the room was so dense with professional achievement that any speaker would need to be at the tiptop of their game or these men and women would scoff them right off the stage. Really, it was that challenging.

Here, too, I was invited to lunch.

But the audience and I had just shared one of the most enjoyable Q & A's I've ever had the pleasure of participating in, so after signing copies, I headed for the door. I wanted to leave on a positive note, let my thoughts sort themselves out privately. Sail through un-scathed.

With experience comes a wealth of awareness.

And once you know something true about yourself, you can't just delete it, it's not possible. Your insides do not believe the lie you are trying to tell yourself.

So I've decided that eating with perfect strangers, after giving so much of myself *to* them, does little for any of us.

They need to believe in the person I was Up There.

And I need to believe that whatever I said Up There is possible.

Blissfully alone, I ate around the corner at Tulio's.

THANK YOU

AND BY "YOU" I mean those of you who take the time to read my column.

Without you, I would not have such a timely reason to compose whatever thoughts are taking up good (or not-so-good) space in my head.

But there is another reason I am grateful.

The biggest downside to being a writer is isolation. It's a lonely job. There is no holiday party (maybe there is for staff writers, but *I'm* not invited), no camaraderie, no other physical presence but the voice inside my mind.

And she can be a real pain sometimes.

I do have email relationships with editors that go back years. Our loyalty is a rare and wonderful thing. But we do not meet for lunch. We do not look intently from across the table and nod with compassion when one of us complains about the size of our paycheck that would barely *cover* lunch.

So, in that sense, you are my only co-workers. And I've stayed with you all these years because it's a quick turnaround, this genre is. I write for you on Sunday and you read me on, what, Wednesday?

Imagine.

Especially considering how many years go into writing a book.

Plus, *gasp*, in the business of book writing my titles are labeled "literary." Meaning I tend to write in complete sentences which is not the least bit chic these days.

But I cannot settle for less. I won't. It would break me.

And if it is true that we create our own heartache through expectation, well, I may need to learn this lesson all over again as I sit here at my desk tweaking every page of *this* book, every paragraph, every word. And once the book is out, it will fall short of my expectations. *I* will fall short.

Fortunately, it may be another year before it even goes to press. So, for now, I am saved from the heaven/hell of getting my hopes up too high. Which leaves me with no real news to share with friends and family who will pass around images of the next generation and I'll be reminded that the world is divided between those who give birth to babies and those who deliver manuscripts.

Though you don't have to be philosophical to see how both tear right through you, cry out for attention at three in the morning, and raising them is hard, thankless work that leaves you feeling like a failure. How dare they disrespect us. Take advantage. Let us down. After all we have sacrificed!

But we forgive them. We always forgive them.

Love is so complicated.

And love is exactly what it is. Since if they are taken from us for any extended amount of time, we desperately want them back.

We would kill to get them back.

Anyway, I want to thank anyone who has made me feel less alone, to the point of preoccupation sometimes.

But preoccupation is good if it helps us to express gratefulness, right?

Rereading that last line makes me remember the phrase that helped me through my twenties, thirties, forties, and right up until now—*the feelings we feed are the ones that grow.*

SHE IS ME

I JUST GOT OFF THE PHONE with the event programmer for the Fine Arts Center in Port Angeles. "So," she said, "what would you talk *about*?"

"I ..." but before I could answer she interrupted to ask what most programmers really want to know, "Would you need to be paid?"

Pause.

So now I will have to find a way to say that while money is not the main thing that drives me, I need to be paid *something*. Which may sound easy, but it's the hardest thing. "Let me begin by answering your first question," I say. "Mainly, I talk about the discipline you need to stay with it."

"Oh, that's good," she says.

"I also like to talk about the business side of things. Which trends to follow but not cater to. What tone to strike when trying to persuade an agent. Or an editor. Or a programmer. Like you," I say with a laugh.

I worry a little when I don't hear a response.

Therefore, I decide *not* to mention other topics I like to cover if time allows: the already successful writers afraid to let anyone new in. Academics believing that creative success belongs only to their colleagues—I don't teach at a college? *Heavens.* The corporate mindset of bringing every decision to the table so that decision-by-consensus ends any progress I'd managed to make with the one member of the board I finally convinced after months, and in some cases, *years*, of soliciting. "I like to talk about how persistent we need to be, how we have to make our own success," is how I put it, finally, leaving out how I feel *after* talking with someone with all the power and connections to help me reach my next goal. How I have to steady myself because I don't quite recognize the woman in the mirror who gathered up the courage to make the call in the first place.

But there she is. And she is me.

I considered the long drive to Port Angeles, the cost of the ferry, the gas. "What is your budget?" I ask, knowing full well that another truth, possibly the truest truth, is that I will have to settle for less money. And that once we hang up, I'll worry if I quoted too high a price, or too little, if I said the right things, or scared her off.

This is when a good long walk is in order.

If at home, I would need to circle Green Lake or stroll along Puget Sound's edge.

But I am not at home. I am writing this to the sound of doves cooing, feeling like the luckiest writer alive because another Art Center *did* hire me, The Donkey Mill Art Center on the Big Island of Hawaii, where my walk will be through a coffee plantation to arrive where thirty people have signed up to give the gift of their precious time.

We will face each other.
And I will begin.

Moon Glow

EVEN IF I CONSIDER PICKING dead leaves off potted succulents "gardening" these days, I have a friend who does not. "Succulents hardly qualify," she says. "They need no maintenance whatsoever."

To which I reply, "Exactly."

She is one of my friends, and I have a few, who has sizable grounds and likes to tease me about calling my tiny balcony a garden. To her, a huge house and garden means she has arrived. But I am lost in all that space.

"Like plants," I say, "we tend to gravitate toward people who don't give us a hard time." She frowns, but her eyes smile. The first time I noticed this smile it filled my appreciation with warm air. It has moved us along ever since.

She came by to drive me, along with three others, up to Skagit Valley, and every one of us is excited about getting out of the city. Just the thought of traveling to farm country cancels every guilty thought I have about playing hooky on a weekday.

Sometimes I wonder how such guilt is even possible.

"We're ahead of the tulips," she says. "We'll be anticipating the color."

I love the idea of imagining a valley full of red and yellow, not to mention how five of us will fit into a Mazda2.

"You're riding shotgun," she says, and off we go.

No sooner are we on the freeway when one of us lights up a little, as she put it, "non-habit-forming inducement."

"But you smoke that stuff every day," I say.

"Your point being?"

"No point."

"It's not like I'm *addicted*."

Fortunately, we all laugh. None of us really wants to be reminded of ourselves, we simply want to *be* ourselves. We are middle-aged women and thank goodness we have middle-aged acceptance of our vices.

Of which there are a few.

Farmland, now on both sides of the freeway, makes me remember a time, early into my marriage, when I planted a container of Night Blooming Jasmine against my husband's advice. I thought that if I placed it close enough to the house it would absorb the reflected heat and eventually trellis over the doorway. "There are pictures," I said, handing him a magazine. "Look."

He thumbed through the pages, shaking his head.

The next day I bought what he called my "potted pipe dream." It lasted right up till our first freeze.

Undaunted, I bought more and more plants, more and more seeds. Particularly, Nasturtium seeds. I scattered them everywhere because this is how I like to spread seeds, a little recklessly.

I think of that haphazard garden often.

Really, the memory of living in that house is nothing without that garden.

I recall something else my husband said, how some women are turned on by strong abs, others by wealth and power, and others by flower seeds sold in small packets.

It will never be even *remotely* possible that I won't remember him saying that.

I suppose I thought of my garden in the same way I thought of my marriage: in its possibility, I found protection. That garden was a metaphor for a lot of my longings and discoveries at the time. But I hardly saw it like that. I was still so blasé about what nature has to teach us.

We even believed that a sense of place might lie in that house. But we were sailors once—our first two homes were sailboats—and I think we were drawn to a floating lifestyle because we had always thought of home as something more fluid than four walls. After a while, the house began to feel like too heavy an anchor that tied us to something we no longer recognized as "us."

One last thought: Like my friends, gardening taught me a lot about acceptance.

For instance, there is conceding acceptance, like when to listen to beds when they cry "let me be!" Livid acceptance when deer munch every seedling to the ground. And frustrated acceptance when tomatoes do a pretty good job of pretending they will ever ripen. Eventually came future acceptance when I had to leave that garden behind in order to dig into new possibilities.

Possibilities.

There it is again. That word.

And why, in La Conner, I buy a succulent called Moon *Glow*. The sign says the plant is well-suited for small spaces in that it likes to spread out but is not aggressive.

I read that sign again.

I had been swept back in time for the last forty minutes. I thought the best choice would be to choose the present.

Exactly where I am. Now.

The Paintings

For years, I went around thinking that I am not one of those people who loves to visit art galleries, that I prefer an artist's studio, where not only the work, but the life of the artist is visible.

Really, the last time I visited a studio, it was *all* there. It not only reeked of paint fumes but of cigarette stubs, stale beer, emptied wine bottles. I thought, *this is what I'm talking about. Dependency is so revealing.*

But there were so many bottles and so many stubs, plus a collection of bongs and feathered roach clips, that I began to see how addiction is no easier on the senses inside of a creative space than out.

Still, this is not what changed my mind about galleries. That happened quite by accident.

I'd wanted to take a stroll through Volunteer Park, that's all. Clear my head. But there were so many people coming and going from the Asian Art Museum that I quickly decided how I would spend the rest of the afternoon.

See, the night before I'd driven all the way to Bellingham to read from my new book and only a hand full of people showed up at the bookstore, two of which kept talking to each other during my reading so that I wanted to gently lift the podium up and pound it down on their heads. "Do it," the voice inside of me said. "I dare you."

To briefly paraphrase the write-up of the show, *Hometown Boy: Liu Xiaodong, one of China's most celebrated artists, grew up in a small town before moving to Beijing. After three decades of experiencing unbridled growth, he returned home. Feeling like an outsider, he masterfully captured the details of daily life in a typical Chinese town.*

I think that's what got me the most, the feeling of wanting to return to the town of our youth. Especially when the city around me has become an ever-changing skyline of tower cranes, one looking as if it might swing through my bedroom window in the slightest wind.

Whenever I try to describe how my neighborhood used to feel, pre-Amazon, compared to how it feels now—a steely vision of man's need to reach higher and higher—I'm always reminded of a woman I know. So much of her face has been lasered or chemically peeled or whatever her "procedures" are called that nothing about her expression seems grounded to the rest of her. She has lost all perspective. She can no longer recognize the difference between what she perceives as youthful, and plain old keeping up with what she can afford— because she is filthy rich.

Anyway, I was so moved by Liu's paintings, I decided to spend the next day in *my* old hometown, Port Townsend, where, in the first years after moving to the city, I couldn't visit without my past crashing into my present, and my future feeling mashed in between.

So, I stopped going back.

Today, I enjoy returning. I like to say I came of age in Port Townsend before I came of middle age in Seattle. And as soon as I see the conical roof of the Manresa Castle that is like a line of delineation between Port Townsend and the rest of the world, it's as if I am tending to my history with a deeper sense of the word.

And yet I am no longer at home. Like Liu, I feel like an outsider. An observer.

In the city, my days are full of work, mostly work, and sometimes, to slow things down a bit, I like nothing more than to cross the Sound and leisurely drive back to a gentler pace, a town that keeps me in touch with how slowly some things shift.

Yet, both worlds remind me how unsettled life can feel.

How restless I often was in that small town, where I spent way too much time telling myself that I was happy. While my insides echoed, *no you are not.*

And while echoes smack of truth, longings seep in more slowly to remind us what *could* be true. And what my longings keep telling me is that reaching for my next goal is a huge part of who I am.

Now, when I'm standing on the ferry deck and looking back at Seattle, I can see how I challenged myself to grow in a hyper-competitive city, learned how to test my limits in ways I never believed possible, which likely comes close to what people mean when they say you are making your dreams come true.

Except they are not dreams. They are, as I said, longings. I am making my longings come true. Trying, anyway.

In Liu's paintings, I see the connections between the younger man he was, and his current strengths. I was so elated that I ran down the steps of the museum feeling as if I had just relived my own transition.

And I guess it might be too much to say his show "changed my life." Or that any show can instantly change your view of failure and success.

Except it did, it completely changed my view of failure and success. And it always feels like a stroke of luck when this happens, when everything about choices made feels satisfying and right.

And for a lack of better words, *worth it.*

LIFTED

My friend D. died.

After struggling for years, he just couldn't struggle anymore.

And I've delayed too long trying to find the words to pay proper tribute. The responsibility scares me to *death*.

Oh. Maybe I should have found another way to say that.

But D. would have laughed. Every single time I stuck my foot in my mouth D. laughed. Then he'd kiss the air on both sides of my head.

I have always needed to shape some kind of a story out of my worst sufferings. When I feel the most vulnerable, *this* is when I write for hours until I feel centered rather than adrift.

Honestly, I feel adrift a lot of the time, though I rarely admit it, even to myself.

And it's such demanding work, centering yourself. Right up until you remember how mercifully a day can turn around if you keep at it.

Now, as I was saying, we lost D. And I thought I'd found a good beginning. But I'm no closer to telling you about *him*.

The Next Day

The last time I saw D. he had been working on choreography somewhere in California. Santa Cruz, I think he said. Mostly, I remember the look in his eyes. A look that refuses to remember how difficult performance is because we are always more passionate about the process, the rehearsals, the *getting there*. We used to joke that being a choreographer is like giving birth. If we remembered the agony, we'd never go near a stage again.

After he left, I could have called to see how things were going, but it was more fun to speculate and hear about it later, once we were together sipping a glass of wine, when everything he said was probably a little more heightened than what he'd actually been through. Which, of course, is the point of sharing a glass of wine.

There are many things that make someone a good performer, but there is one that always stands out: heart. And D. had the heart to let his audience not only feel the energy expanding inside of him, but inside of *them*. From the moment the lights came up, his energy would absolutely grab you.

And the golden rule of performance is that it has to grab you.

To watch D. perform was like eyeing a natural phenomenon.

"You're amazing!" I yelled to him once, over the roar of the audience. I was waiting in the wings, trying not to bump into the dancers as they came flying off stage. "I *know!*" he shouted back, and then he ran back out to take another bow. He was so proud that night. Like me, dancing was the largest part of the image D. had of himself.

We hardly agreed about everything, though, not even close. Disagreements came often. And they were always intense, always justified, always his best ideas clashing with my own until he would say that while he appreciated my idea, he liked his better.

And nine times out of ten, his was better. I knew it.

But it was more than that. I was still trying to figure out which demands of the business of dance made me feel more connected to the process, and which ones made me feel less, which made them easier to hand over.

One other thing comes to mind. What D. and I shared was being wholly involved in our work, a luxury not everyone can claim. And sometimes, I like to imagine what the world would be like if everyone was able to work this way.

Okay, this *has* been a good beginning. Good enough to balance on. For now.

Composed, fully en pointe, *lifted*.

Oso

—For Steve and Theresa Harris

ASK A WRITER HOW THEY DECIDE what to write and they might just shrug their shoulders.

If you press them about it, they may even rely on a cliché: *it's as if the words write me, not the other way around.*

It's a way of describing the process that I am wary of, but I do fall into it.

Because it is true.

Take today. I started to write about my neighbor who thinks a woman president would be a disaster. "Do not say that!" I screamed, turning my back on him. It made me feel better, to yell at him, better than I'd felt in days.

Then, just like that, the dream I had about *Bertha* sprang to mind, where she resumes digging the SR 99 tunnel under the Alaskan Way Viaduct, burrows her way into Elliott Bay and swims off for good . . . prompting me to check my emails.

Only to get this sunken feeling.

Something didn't seem quite right about my friend Amargit's last email, and this one feels even worse. Though it does occur to me that it is simply an *Oso.*

Or what I've come to refer to as an *Oso*.

You see, my husband used to work with a naval architect named Steve Harris who was, "the most honest guy in the world," according to Larry. So naturally, he wanted to work with Steve again. So he called Steve. In fact, he *kept* calling Steve. Steve never called back. "He was always quick to return my call," Larry said.

So Larry built this whole thing up in his mind, how Steve no longer wanted to work with him, how he must have said or did something wrong, offended him somehow. He lost sleep over it. He couldn't figure out why Steve wouldn't get back to him. Then he heard that Steve and his wife had been tending their weekend cabin in Oso, Washington when a massive landslide hit.

I'm afraid another predictable cliché comes to mind here: *They never knew what hit them.*

In one email, Amargit cancelled dinner. In the next, lunch. Now, even more troubling, she is calling off our weekly walk around the sale racks downtown.

There are so many ways to reach out lately. Should I call? Send another email? Text? Facebook? It's too much!

For whatever reason, pivotal things come to me late in life. My wisdom teeth came in my thirties. My best girlfriend in my forties; not in high school, not in college. And my best insights are just coming to me now: it is ego that makes us think that another person's actions have anything to do with *us*.

I spent another few hours wondering if Amargit was through with me. I found my husband early on, but I've definitely felt the pain of a friendship breakup over the years. Mending hurt feelings is the hardest work there is. I could see, or thought I could see, the writing on the wall.

But as soon as I let that image emerge, another one reached in and smacked it flat against the wall.

I picked up the phone.

Maybe I called because I was afraid to, and I don't like being afraid, and nothing makes me more afraid than hearing someone refer to "talking" as "old-school." Only by speaking my fears aloud do I feel even *close* to hopeful again.

"Maaareee Luuu, I am *so* embarrassed," she said as soon as she heard my voice, a confession delivered two seconds before I said, "I'll be right over." Talk about old-school. Talk about reassuring and comforting and exactly right. I got in my car.

And it was a relief to know that my friend and I were fine, though there would be time ahead that wouldn't feel fine at all.

Why?

Because she had one of those botched chemical peels that goes horribly wrong. (Why, why do we do this? As *if* we can peel away time.) She was "in hiding," she said. She was depressed. She got the peel, *gasp*, "on sale." She was trying to find a dermatologist to fix her face.

The whole way over I wondered what it felt like to have to find someone to *fix your face*.

When she met me at the door, she wore a shawl over part of her face. She's from India, so it didn't look as funny as if, say, I wore a shawl over part of my face. It was blue, made of silk, or one of those new fabrics that mimics silk, but the point is, I would miss her terribly if she was not in my life.

So, Steve, I write this for one simple reason: I want you to know that Larry gathered strength from your friendship, that he had always preferred working alone until he met you. I saw loss in his eyes, deep loss, when he discovered yet again how quickly everything can change. He looked bewildered, suddenly, and exhausted.

I want you to know there were red dents between his eyes where his sunglasses had pressed in, before he removed them to shake his head and cry.

I want you to know that his tears made me feel miserable in the happiest imaginable way.

My New Friend

NOTHING MAKES SOMEONE TRUST you more than when you promise something and then you *keep* your promise.

So when My New Friend—she and I met in a grief-counseling session—said it was okay to share her story but *not* her name, well, I am doing just that.

It was nearly a year after I lost my mother when I decided to show up to the support group recommended by the hospice nurse that helped me through the most overwhelming year of my life. "One of the worst times is around six months *after* your loss," she said. "This is when people stop asking how you are, and you are left alone with your grief."

It was like hearing, as they say, *the strike of a chord.*

The last time I called one of my oldest friends, she avoided the subject of my mother altogether. I had the distinct feeling she couldn't, or wouldn't, allow herself to ask how I was doing because it made her too uncomfortable. Maybe she thought I was okay because *I* didn't mention my mother. I mean, our conversations didn't generally include our mothers, neither of us brought them up. In one way it felt as if we'd outgrown the need to. In another, it was a relief to talk about anything else since, no doubt, one of them was making us crazy at the moment and we'd never outgrow *that*.

But even if your friends don't ask, grief spills out unexpectedly. The other night when I saw an ad to market phones to kids still strapped into car seats, it made me cry. "It's the end of all innocence!" I sobbed. When what I was really feeling was the loss of, sniff-sniff, my own.

And I knew there was something seriously wrong when even our sunny weather didn't cheer me up. Sunshine usually boots the blues right out.

I knew it again when I learned that my new book was to be published and I was, like, *oh, wow, great*. I was not excited, just accepting.

Nothing about my days felt right, there was always a snag.

So when it was my turn to share with the group, I told everyone how my mother used to smoke all the time and how she lied about it to her sister and to my father, and how I'd once overheard her say that without a cigarette, she felt like less of herself. And how much it bothered me that she needed something so bad for her to feel good about herself. I don't know why I thought to tell this particular story to a group of strangers, or why I thought it would help me feel better, but everyone said I was just so *honest*.

And that did help. Some.

Next, My New Friend spoke.

And it was there, in a conference room in a public library, that I encountered a whole new level of courage, grief, and survival. The room went still. At one point, I felt like I didn't know how to do it, how to listen to the level of anguish she described. At another, I didn't want to be me anymore, or anyone like me, I wanted to be *her*.

Here is some of what she said, "Two skinheads beat my twenty-year old son up in our mobile home park in the San Jacinto Valley. They stomped and kicked him in the head. He now resides in a long-term care facility with permanent brain damage."

How do you *not* stand and throw your arms around someone sharing a loss like this? No matter how long I live in Seattle, I will never get the hang of social reserve. I know people like me are one of the lesser problems of a grief-counselor's duties, but she did eventually have to remind me to sit back down.

When My New Friend was finished, she thanked us for listening and handed out homemade cookies to pass around. All I could think was *why is it that the one who has lost the most is the one who remembers to bring a gift for everyone else?*

When the session ended, My New Friend and I talked again in the parking lot. "My son is gay *and* Hispanic," she said.

Her words lingered.

I got to thinking about my friends Wade and Dennis. How I'd stood in line with them at the new-at-the-time Queen Anne Trader Joe's. They looked on top of the world holding hands, despite the stare from an elderly woman behind us. Except she wasn't staring in a hateful way, but the way you might expect a woman in her eighties to stare at two men holding hands, not like something that could haunt her forever, but more of a startle to witness, up close, an outwardly gay couple for the first time.

Before a smile came over her.

The more I studied that smile, the more I knew it was genuine. And I believe that, underneath it, what she recognized in Wade and Dennis was love and what she loved about love, any love, all love.

It was like witnessing time evolve as it should. It was breathtaking.

Nearly as breathtaking as when My New Friend said, "I have forgiven the men who hurt my son."

Sugar Birds

THE NEXT TIME I'M IN Whole Foods and someone is reading a food label as if studying a dissertation, I want to remember this moment: I am in a tiny bodega in Frederiksted on the island of St. Croix. My vegetable choices are limited. There are onions and there are potatoes. Both are moldy.

St. Croix is one of three American Virgin Islands. "*This* island," one of the staff of the Caribbean Museum Center for the Arts (where I'm to be writer-in-residence for two weeks) says on my first day, "is the rougher of the three. If you want touristy, you fly to St. Thomas. If you want upscale, you go to St. John. *Here* you need to watch yourself."

"Okay," I say.

"You might hear gunfire but don't worry, the gangs keep to themselves."

"Oh." I hadn't even unpacked yet.

"Use mosquito repellent, there's Dengue Fever."

"Hmm." I look down at the mosquito bites already ringing my ankles like little red beads on a bracelet.

"And we're sorry, but the air-conditioner in your room is broken, someone stole the copper compressor tubing."

Oh shiiiii... "Um. Okay," I say, dreading the Caribbean sun beating into my room when I try to work or sleep.

A bit of history: Frederiksted or "Freedom City" is named for the emancipated slaves from the sugar plantations who settled here. The ruins of the sugar mills, raised between 1750 and 1800 when the island was under Danish rule and one of the richest sugar producing islands in all of the Caribbean, now serve as reminders of the ruthless history of the island and the lives of abuse the slaves suffered in the cane fields.

No one can put the truth of sugar's history behind them here, certainly not me, and deep down I can't help but wonder if some of the residents who live fifteen miles east in the only other town on the island, Christiansted, are okay with this.

I have 257 pages of new editorial notes to flush out. Completing a book is, well, I was about to say "brutal," but I will have to find another word now that I'm surrounded by so many strong reminders of the real thing.

Once my work is done for the day, I walk town, every dilapidated alley, into the heart of daily life: food smells, children's voices, TV in the background, dishes clanking. All of it brings such familiar, primal comfort, tears spring to my eyes.

By night, I teach dance in the universally identical local ballet studio: floor, mirrors, barre. No matter where I find myself in the world, dancing is still the quickest, easiest way of belonging.

"What kind of dance will you teach?" one parent asks, lightheartedly, "ballet, contemporary, imperialist? Ha ha ha."

There is so much truth in her question. Which is why I laugh, too.

And not to change the subject too abruptly but remember Darwin's Beak of the Finch theory? One of the most fascinating things I discover on St. Croix is this theory in action. There is a variety of finch the locals call "sugar birds." In nature, the bird is an insect eater, but the ones on St. Croix had modified their beaks within a few dozen generations to scoop up the sugar that was spilled around the mills.

One of these finches comes to my picnic table. Its bill is formed into a half-circle to feed on the granulated sugar people still put out for them especially when a cruise ship docks for the day.

The finch turns its head sideways, lays it flat on the table, and rakes the scattered granules into a tiny pile it can spoon up. When three men walk up to my table from the cruise ship dock, one of them cries, "Hey, check it out!"

The bird flies off.

The sugar remains.

I look down at my hands. I know to avoid direct eye contact with the men. But when—despite the little handwritten sign explaining the birds—one of them puts a cigarette out in the small mound of sugar, I say, "Nice," without looking up, adding to my sense of inse- curity, but I can't help that.

The men laugh at my insult. They laugh at *me*. When one of them calls me a *bicha* under his breath, I am stung, even though I started it.

I really need a thicker skin. That was the motto of all my days in St. Croix.

"Please don't tell me you told them off," Larry says when I tell him the story. "Don't make me worry about you any more than I already do."

One of the things I initially enjoy the most, but after just one day *miss* the most, is the everyday of Larry and me.

Marriage, *our* marriage—well, yes, he really ticks me off sometimes, and I can make him *so* mad, oh, you should just see the steam come out of his ears if I even suggest he is anything at *all* like his mother, which is just so true of any one of us—is a love unprecedented nowadays. I don't want to take it for granted.

Even though I do sometimes.

But it's at the top of my list of what I want to change when I get home.

God, I am so homesick.

Salute!

I haven't been to a real dinner party in ages, so I am thrilled to be invited to one by friends who live in Blue Ridge.

I write a lot about my friends, I know, but I love them, *and* they fascinate me.

The first thing I notice walking up to the front door are flowering shrubs that frame the footpath. My friends take a lot of pride in keeping a lovely yard. I take it as a good sign that the food will not be ready-made party trays from Costco.

I know the reason we come together is not solely for the food, but I've decided that there are just too many party trays out there that look like fun but are not. Even if the rest of the world is happy with spicy chicken wings, I think we should at least *try* to make something when we entertain—stuffed shells or a lasagna—and not drink too much until it is out of the oven.

The other thing that gave me pause about the house was how much space there is around it. This happens whenever I leave the city. And I know people still call this far north "the city," but nothing could feel further from the truth. The next house feels positively *distant*.

To see so much space, that so much space *exists,* well, I cannot stop smiling.

I am not sure what my smile means.

Because in my neighborhood that I like (occasionally even love), we are so tightly packed together. What this means is that in order to maintain any sense of privacy, we live further apart, emotionally. And since everyone whips out their phone to pretend to be otherwise engaged should any opportunity for neighborly interaction present itself, detachment has gotten a whole lot easier.

But in the space of a thirty-minute Lyft ride, the world completely changes.

What is this? A complete stranger waves to me from her window? *Hello.*

Now, shoot, *I* want a yard and cushy chaise lounges set out in the sun. And shrubs.

I didn't imagine myself staying in Belltown, but grassy neighborhoods have become so expensive, my house dreams are on hold. I'd have to move to Centralia.

My house-envy eventually eases, it always eases.

Especially when I remember how that friendly wave from the neighbor next door also means she is noting my every move. And that as soon as I get home, I will share a glass of wine on the rooftop with *my* neighbor, Stephanie, and how after only a few sips I will probably say quietly to myself, "thank you." I will not even know who I am thanking exactly, myself, Stephanie, or my good fate. But I will feel so suddenly grateful I will just need to say so.

So, back in Blue Ridge . . .

There are seven of us at the table. One couple lives on Queen Anne. "*Upper* Queen Anne." One woman is from Burien. "*Old* Burien." You can tell how much the distinctions mean to them. One lives on "The East Side," meaning Bellevue or Redmond or why doesn't he just say? And there is the host and his partner, and, because Larry is out of town, there is me. We have come to celebrate our hosts' Silver Anniversary. Despite the legal battle their union has been over the years, these guys have more of a marriage than most couples I know. It is easy to feel their devotion. "We bought this house nineteen years ago," one says, "before Seattle went crazy."

I am a little touchy about being part of the "crazy" he is referring to. I know he doesn't like all the condos springing up. He calls our 500 square feet a "cage." The first (and only) time he visited, he actually laughed out loud. "But you are *adults!*" he cried.

More wine is poured. I am not the only Italian, so we are very animated by now.

I look out the window. "Sweeping views of the ocean always move me," I say.

"That's because you live in a cage."

"That didn't take long." And to myself, I add, *yes. And no.*

Yes, because my "cage" is not perched over the sound with a bird's eye view of ninety percent of the world's trade passing by in shipping containers. No, in that I do not let myself long for such a view. I could not pay the taxes, let alone the mortgage.

Apparently, no one but me can say the word "condo" without smirking. Everyone agrees they need more space.

Space. I remember thinking about it a lot when I first moved to Seattle because, to me, it still had so much of it. But instead of saying anything, I do something so unlike me. I just listen. "I won't go anywhere near downtown anymore," the woman from Burien says.

Oh god. Now everyone is digging deep into memories of "old" downtown. Mama's Kitchen and concerts on Pier 62.

I don't say that, *hello*, I'm the only one who actually lives downtown. I do say, "But we can walk everywhere. When was the last time you walked to the grocery store?"

Oh, no. That didn't go over well. Everyone is overweight. Two of them, seriously.

"Well," the woman from Burien says, "I grew up in this city and . . ."

I find people who start off this way are just wanting to go back in time with more nostalgia than fact. ". . . how people can live like ants in a hive is beyond me."

She means bees. Or an anthill. I don't dare say.

I do want to say that no one can hold on to the past. That we have to accept our friends and family as they grow, change, hurt our feelings, make us mad, and how it is the same with a city. And I was pretty close to doing so until someone fires up a leaf blower next door so that our host races outside to yell, "Use a rake for chrissakes!"

Knowing him as I do, he just needed to yell at *some*one. No host should feel upset about the way his dinner is going, so *I* yell, "Salute!" And now that I have everyone's attention, I raise my glass.

"Salute!" everyone cheers. We take a sip, the lasagna arrives.

Lasagna! I just love these guys.

Plus, there are wonderful smells of something sweet baking. Homemade dessert, too? Can you believe it?

Finalmente ci ritroviamo insieme in amicizia, in pace.

Finally we find ourselves together in friendship. In peace.

SAVOR

I'VE NEVER BEEN THE KIND OF PERSON who can wait to open a gift that arrives early, certainly not a Little Christmas gift.

More commonly known to the rest of the world as the Feast of the Epiphany, Little Christmas falls on January 6th, and in my childhood home it was the official end of the holiday season. Likely why it brought relief to my mother's eyes.

Eyes speak. And parents never know which look is going to be the one their kids will remember forever.

We always saved our smallest-sized gift to open on Little Christmas. After the oohing and aahing, the tree came down—faster if we could get dad to help.

Last week, when my Little Christmas gift arrived in the mail, it was like having our family ritual all over again. I couldn't wait to open it. I sat down on the floor and tore into the tiny box.

Earrings! My friend Lena knows who I am.

I didn't know what the greenish-blue stone was at first, but I learned that aquamarine, in ancient lore, is believed to be the treasure of mermaids.

I love that. No one is more of a mermaid than me, and I am fairly confident this is why she chose the stone.

I joined a health club with a pool. I swim every day, no matter how cold. No matter how rainy. Lena thinks I'm crazy and I am. I am crazy for swimming.

In the water, my heart is light.

In the water, I convince myself that, say, criticism does not dwarf a compliment, things of that nature.

If I stay in long enough, I am (nearly) able to forgive everyone and everything that has ever hurt me. Exactly how and why this happens hasn't been fully explained to me, but that's fine. Because it doesn't last. Once I towel off, all resentments resume to normal.

I take a moment to try on the earrings and pull my hair back in a ponytail to show them off. They are earrings you would wear to, hmm, let's see . . . a Feast of the Epiphany!

Or, wait, I know. Out for a pizza at Serious Pie.

My friend Lena has always had the gift of timing. This was true even when we shared a room in college. She was the one who remembered to whip out the Visine when we had to sneak by our dorm monitor past curfew. And when, as a freshman, I had the flu, it was Lena who made me tea. The strongest sensation I remember isn't how sick I was, or even the fear I had because it was the first week of a new semester, but the safety I felt under Lena's care.

We don't remember the days, weeks, and years, thoroughly. What stays with us is the care we receive when we need it the most. When we are young, we assume there will be so many of these totally supportive acts, too many to recall. Until we realize that there aren't so many, really. And how important it is to relish each and every one.

I tried to be better at relishing last year, but improvement can take a long time. Not biblically long. But a while.

And even if I wasn't fully conscious of any real headway—in the form of taking enough time to properly relish—I knew I was feeling something improved, even if I didn't have the words for it yet.

Until I did.

And they are not even *close* to original. I've heard them all my life. But they are wise. Oh, they are wise: *Take a breath. Savor the moment.*

Noticed

After the third shooting this week, I lost the capacity for emotional response. I may glance at the screen, but I am not allowing the images in. I am unable to process another tragedy after so many. I am numb.

There are certain detachments we surrender to. In order to cope.

On the surface I'm okay, but I am haunted by how the innocent bystander at Third & Pine must have felt in her last moments. I think I will never be able to make peace with this image.

One of my friends said she has stopped turning on the news. "I am less and less armored against the horrors," she said.

I go to bed at night worried. I want our city officials to act. I *scream* at them to act, that's how far gone I am. I am desperate for our downtown to feel like less of a drug zone. Less of a drug *camp*.

The night after the shooting, instead of clearing the dishes I sat staring out the window. And who knows why memories come to us when they do, but I told my husband how one of the finest compliments I've ever received came from a poet who was also a Catholic nun: Madeline DeFrees. She said that I had the soul of a non-conformist. "I will never forget how humble she was," I said, which is something I always admire in another.

To avoid thinking about the nine-year old boy who was also shot, I went on to say how many of the poets I knew in those days were *not* humble. In fact, they had egos. Big egos. "Greenhouse-strawberry big," I said. I talked on and on that night. I was trying to free the lump in my throat. The dishes never made it to the sink.

The next day I had to take time off from my desk, from shouldering-guilt-that-does- not-belong-to-me. Neither of which I am particularly good at.

The best way for me to do this is to get outside where people are talking about, oh, I don't know, how about those Seahawks?

The first man I see wears a Seahawks jacket and a Seahawks cap. He is very Seahawks, this man. "You're very supportive," I say.

That's all I said. But I felt better already.

In the Sculpture Park, I spot a woman who clearly needs a hand getting down the concrete steps. She is fit and fashionably dressed. And for a second, I thought she was much younger, but when she lifted her head it was clear she was in her eighties.

Her clothes, however, *were* younger. But not as if she is trying to look younger, just that maybe she likes to keep up, pay attention. She wore a long, asymmetrical sweater over black skinny jeans.

"You look lovely," I said.

She came right back with, "Well, I do like to shop. Too much so, according to my husband." She smiled.

I smiled too. But what really moved me is how quickly she responded. I remember my mother telling me that she longed to talk to people more in her later years but that it didn't happen much anymore. "Most people don't want to talk to an old lady," she said. "I'm finding it harder and harder to go out."

I'm telling you, those words were like a knife to my heart.

I said to the woman, "You're not one of those women who take their husbands shopping with you, I hope."

"He's gone now," she said. "But we had a good marriage, right up until the cancer."

I listened. She talked. I talked. She listened.

And today as I remember her, what she really loved is being included. Conversation helps us out of our heads and into the immediate present. A much better place than spending too much time alone with our fears.

Because, let's face it, the shootings will not let up. There are too many guns.

I think this may be just about the saddest thing I have ever said.

I need to leave my desk again.

I need to let the city wash over me.

I—well, *we*—need to find a way to trust these sidewalks again.

CLARA-FIED

FOR AS LONG AS I CAN REMEMBER, I've been wanting to write about Clara Rhodefer. I've been putting it off for over a decade because, for one thing, my fondest memory of her has to do with watering my vegetable garden, and I haven't watered a vegetable garden in far too long.

For another, I didn't want to write a story about Clara that she could read. Clara was a very private person.

My husband and I used to rent a cabin on her property, better known in Sequim as The Old Rhodefer Farm. A large white house, Clara's home, overlooks the rest of the land, including the one-room cabin we lived in, and one month we came up short of cash so Clara suggested we paint the cabin in lieu of rent.

About a week later, with scaffolding strewn around the yard, Larry and I stood staring at our freshly painted home, Clara joining us for once. She'd pretty much ignored us until then, but she kept looking down at my garden instead of at the cabin. Placing her hands on her hips, she looked directly at my pole beans and said, "Well, from *here* they don't look so bad."

How many people would say such a thing?

I guess she felt she should have a say in whatever goes on next door. But her comment was nothing compared to the approval I felt when she finally walked over to stand with us. I felt our out-of-town-ness was finally being accepted, that *we* were finally being accepted. I stepped closer to her.

She looked at me crossly and said, "Mary Lou, there's something I've been meaning to tell you."

I braced myself. Larry put his hand on my shoulder.

"You should water your garden in the morning while the ground is still cool so the roots can handle the cold water."

Was it true?

It didn't matter.

What mattered was that she wanted to share her knowledge and it endeared her to me. Everyone has a desire to reveal what they know to someone who will listen. "But I thought it was better to water in the evening after the sun goes down so," I had to think for a minute, "so the water doesn't evaporate in the heat of the day."

"No. Cold water distresses roots that are still warm from the sun."

Farming know-how has been in Clara's family since Seattle was a logging camp, so I listened. And when she was done, I said the next thing that popped into my head, "Larry said to water in the evening." It was just one of the many, many times I have believed Larry because, well, because he is a man.

As young women, there are so many of these errors in judgement.

Since writing that last sentence, I've decided that a huge part of maturing means that we know to assume that a lot of the time men are just bluffing it. It's like they have been given this bluffing-privilege at birth, permission to *not* know while pretending they *do*. And if they ever admit to bluffing (don't hold your breath) it's a pretty feeble apology, generally.

Hopefully, with time, they will at least gain a sense of humor about bluffing, which works to their advantage. Once they can laugh about it, we more or less forgive them for everything because we want to forgive them. For everything.

Larry looks at me, realizes I have blamed him, and says, "Hey, what do I know?" This made Clara laugh.

From then on, I was happy to take Clara's advice. As instructed, the next morning I watered first thing. "You've been Clara-fied," Larry said.

By the end of August, I had to lift the hose way over my head to reach all of my vegetables. I'd look up and see Clara reading the *Gazette* at her kitchen table, but I knew she was watching me out of the corner of her eye, maybe even thinking what I was thinking—that watering is a great way to start the day.

The best.

For plants and for people.

I stand up from my desk and walk out on my balcony to douse my small flower pots.

But small is good. This was Clara's real message, I think.

Small and continual is good.

MORE

WE HAVE FRIENDSHIPS FOR MANY different reasons—to experience the best in others, to experience the best in ourselves, to find comfort, easy conversation, to better understand our past, present, and where we are headed. And for many of us, this has little to do with reducing our relationships to likes and followers.

We are looking for *more*.

I have terrific women friends. Wise, kind, and fun (for the most part).

And I have Charles.

Charles's most admirable quality is that he is a good listener. "What's on your mind, darling?" he'll say, flashing a smile—which I believe is the most generous way to begin a conversation—before lowering his gaze as if he's about to hear one of life's sacred secrets.

Or, you know, whatever is bothering me.

A few weeks ago Charles said, "Why do people share everything about themselves? What people *don't* know about us is the most interesting part."

We were talking about how drunk everyone is on selfies, "in the same way the Russians guzzled the vodka," he said, "and look what happened to them."

There are few conversations when, regardless of the subject matter, you sense that all of your thoughts and emotions are aligned with all of your friend's thoughts and emotions and you are *simpatico*. Which is the polar opposite of, say, when the whole exchange feels like a test you can't get right.

Which reminds me of a test I had the other day while waiting in line at Whole Foods. I was chatting with the guy behind me about local lettuce, fruit in season, that kind of thing. Except he kept looking at his phone.

I tried to overlook it, be cool, be current, but I had this crushing sense of being disregarded. And every time this happens, I can't help but feel that we have been duped into believing one reality is never enough because if it were, the world's hottest economy would screech to a crashing halt.

Even now, I think of him talking and scrolling at the same time and I see a gutless way to communicate. I wanted to say, *we do exist without our phones, people, we do! WE are what is real in the world!*

I did come right out and ask him what is so important that he has to be in on it even as he lays produce on the conveyor belt, one of those ridiculous things I hear myself say sometimes, but I say it anyway. And that's when his girlfriend (wife?) jumped in, "This is just how it is now."

As if I knew nothing. As if I don't have an iPhone and know how to use it.

At any rate, she reminded me that since I do have more years behind me, I have attained more success, too, more independence. So I can enjoy a little harmless chitchat, and, okay, a little harmless flirting, without checking in. My flesh may be softer, but my attitude is firm: One shared idea, opinion, or observation can make everything around us seem more, dare I use the word, *connected*.

Why settle for less when the secret of a perfect Marinara sauce—dash of cinnamon, teaspoon of sugar—could be yours without needing to Google it.

And, yes, I may very well be hoping for a miracle. But if you're shopping at Whole Foods you are certainly paying enough for a miracle.

So I say thank goodness for Charles. He is one of the most successful men I know— work he enjoys, a wife he loves, family he adores. Yet, he knows how to leave his phone off for however long it takes. Life may be going on at a hectic pace around us, but he looks into my eyes when he speaks and shows me he'd never let something as expansive as our friendship be dwarfed by something small as a phone.

I'm so happy to know Charles is free to come up to my studio later. He will pick a subject, or I will, and we will lean against the barre.

And we will talk.

ENLIGHTENED

HONESTLY, I DON'T KNOW what to make of some of the things I hear my audiences say.

Heaven knows, it's enlightening to call oneself a "speaker."

Most days I keep my head down and write without giving any thought to who will read my work. This is my freedom, my solitude.

On the opposite side of solitude, there are times when I'm invited to surface in front of my readers. Or, more often, people who have never heard of me *or* my work.

Either way, for the couple of hours we are together, we are close allies. If everything goes well.

Usually it does.

This week I was invited to two entirely different settings to give the same talk about friendship or, basically, how it does a woman good to talk about it.

On Tuesday I addressed women who work in Silicon Valley where the hotel conference room looked over San Francisco Bay. And if I didn't yet know the resonance of *the* most up-to-date sound equipment, I do now. The acoustics were so good that no matter what I said, I felt I knew exactly what I was talking about.

I was in *control*.

I couldn't have planned how good the acoustics would be, or how much more confident they would make me, because I rarely get the opportunity to speak on such a sophisticated stage, technologically. I quickly learned that in the speaking world, there are all the other venues. And there is *this*.

But excuse me if I laugh a little here because I do not begin to think that this kind of opportunity will come along all that often. It's why I need, like water and air, all the less formal venues. They are my constant practice.

Take the old grange hall north of Spokane where, on Saturday, seventy women gathered to hear me speak and I had to work really hard to focus, because even with two wood stoves burning it was so cold inside I couldn't stop shivering. To see over the lectern (a wobbly music stand), I had to climb up on an overturned cardboard box full of jiggling wine bottles while the microphone dangled a foot over my head. Before I went on, I had to walk into the restroom, sit for five minutes in a locked stall to have a little pep talk with myself about how good I am at what I do.

But what struck me as soon as I stepped up to the mike was how much more relaxed this group was with each other. And with me.

My love of good acoustics in nothing compared to my love of relaxed intimacy.

In Silicon Valley, when someone asked about "process," and someone usually does, I said, "there's a lot to be said for just keeping at it day after day," and after watching their reaction for a few seconds, I added something about how people are turning to their phones for everything these days. "But the instant gratification is the opposite of the slow process good writing is, the kind that takes years to complete."

It takes guts to say such a thing in Silicon Valley.

I can say that I saw a few heads nodding. I can also say that I saw a few heads *not* nodding. One woman (in her twenties, I think) stood to say how the corporate world isn't cutting it for her and that her ideas are not valued by the unreceptive men on her team; how even the word "team" is one she rarely trusts anymore. She feels less creative in the tech world, she said, less like herself. "I have no friends. I have no *time* for friends." (Here's where my talk comes into such a conference.) "But I don't know what else to *do*."

"I have heard that the Mad Men of our era wear hoodies," I said, and thank goodness they laughed.

Another admitted she "went a little nuts" before she quit coding. "I went on a bit of a rampage," she said. "Some of the stuff I did I would never have done had I not been at the end of my rope."

A silence fell over the room. As if no one wanted to say what it was she'd done. But everyone *knew*. Except me.

In Spokane, feelings about work relationships were just as passionate. One woman shared how she'd overheard a younger co-worker refer to her as a "geezer" and how she was devastated for days.

I felt for her. When young women poke fun at age as if it diminishes a woman's worth like driving a car off the lot, it spurs the fiercest feelings in me, too.

Before I returned to my car, I took a stroll through the gardens around the grange hall, pleased with how well everything went. Until I heard someone say, "Well, I'll never get *that* hour of my life back."

Are you kidding me? It was the geezer!

Even if I know that there is always the one you can never win over, I'm still talking *mean*. Anyone who says such a thing within earshot of the person they wish to insult, redefines mean.

Fortunately, the woman walking beside her understood the point of the evening, that we need to support each other, not cut each other down. "You're just jealous," she said.

My next move may have happened mostly because she said that. I marched right up to the, ahem, *geezer* and said in a surprisingly calm voice, "I enjoyed meeting you. You've taught me so much."

And because some of the best advice I've ever been given is, "scoffers are just people helping us to grow," I meant it.

CRABS IN A BUCKET

MY OFFICE IS REALLY JUST A LITTLE nook in my living room that doesn't do justice to the word *office*. But it's enough for me.

My famous-writer-friend calls it "cuuute." The number of *u's* in her pronunciation reminds me how well I've learned to do a few things I never thought possible. Like pretend something that really bothers me was never said.

When she phones to ask if I'll look in on her cat while she is teaching at a writer's conference in Prague, I tell her I'm happy to do it, even though jealousy makes me want to hang up on her. My husband is on a business trip and I'm a cat person.

"Sure," I say, trying hard to keep the edge out of my voice.

As soon as I hang up, I slip into a silent funk.

In a word, I am *green*.

I like her. I've always liked her. When I think about her, I'm glad we're friends. As the years go by, I am more and more sure we will remain so. It's a pretty simple question I ask myself lately: Does the thought of her bring a smile to my face?

Yes.

Unless I think of her trust fund status. Then, dang, it can feel as though the green is never going to let up.

Lately, when this happens, I spend half of my time in a swirl of self-doubt while the other half refuses to give in, until I wonder what on *earth* I was so jealous of until I want to kick myself.

I'll never forget the time I was walking the beach by the ferry terminal in Kingston and I came across a fisherman who stuck his hand into a white 5-gallon bucket full of crabs. "Why don't they escape?" I asked.

"They aren't too clever," he said without looking up.

They scratched and scratched against the plastic, clawing over each other to get to the top. But as soon as one almost made it over, the others pulled it back down. I kept wanting them to make a crustacean chain, file up and over the rim until the last lingering crab was safely on the other side.

Huh. I get why those crabs popped into mind just now. I have been caught in the scum of my own bucket. *My* claws are scratching the sides. It is not a pretty sight. "Really?" I hear myself say.

I know jealousy can work as a beacon, steering us toward something we want. But, like gossip, a little is fine, but too much of it and you are one schlep away from small. I don't want to spend one more minute feeling jealous of my friend.

The writer Daniel Gilbert calls this "babysitting our own happiness." The woman within (who babysits *me*) just had to be reminded that "comparing leads to dissatisfaction," words that, ever since they flashed across the screen in the film *Hector and the Search for Happiness*, I try to apply whenever I feel the sides of my bucket closing in.

I love that my friend trusts me with her beloved cat.

What's more, she always takes the time to write a proper thank you note, pen to paper, and you know how much I love that. Such attention to detail, such thoughtfulness, can flush out any lingering stain.

Even the most hideous shade of green.

LAKE COUNTRY

EVERY SO OFTEN I RECEIVE a most unexpected invitation: Would I consider coming to Tower, Minnesota? "We hold our cultural events in a restored train car," the programmer, Nancy, said.

Now, what author wouldn't want to read in a restored train car? "Of course I'll come!" I said. *And* Tower lies at the end of one of the longest paved bike trails in the United States. If I rode 30 to 40 miles a day for four days, I'd be there!

I was met in Grand Rapids, fitted with a bike, and driven to an inn at the trailhead, where I stowed my bag and rushed outside, eager to discuss the trail with the locals.

But the locals weren't so eager *for* me.

"There are bears," my innkeeper said.

"Have you ever seen a bear?" I asked.

"No."

"I have," I say with a smile, remembering inner tubing down the Wenatchee River. The bear chewed its salmon and watched me drift by.

"The wind is against you," her husband said.

True. But it felt like more of a breeze.

Later, when I stopped to ask directions to the trail, a woman standing in her yard said, "There are child molesters hiding out in the woods."

"Since I'm a grown woman, that won't be a problem. Have you ever ridden the trail?"

"No."

And you live next to it? The most fearful, I find, are the ones who have never tried.

At the local bar, my waitress said, "There are wolves."

Noting the eyes of the drunk leering at me from three stools down, I think, *there are always a few wolves to contend with.*

The thing that seemed to bother everyone the most, though, was that I was alone. There are places where people look at me funny when I say that I am traveling alone, and this was one of those places. They look at me even funnier after they ask if I have any kids.

If you are not in the mood for this sort of questioning, you'd better stick to the cities.

Because in Northern Minnesota, with its long history of mining, you do not go off into la la land. You do not want to say, "My work is not just a job, but an expression of what sustains me." And you especially do not want to say, "I could have had kids, but I didn't *want* to."

It can be lonely in the world when you are different. I'm far from letting this bother me. What *does* bother me is how many thinly-veiled ways people find to say, "We don't have Black people here."

The bar's huge TV screen was abuzz with the question of racism after the shooting in Charleston (and all of the other shootings and fatal chokeholds and brutalities). This is where Larry would have kicked me under the table, knowing I was about to ask the two women seated next to me the very same question.

"We're still pretty safe from all *that*," one woman said, reaching for the ketchup. Shaking salt onto her fries, her friend said, "I thank the good Lord every day that we don't have a lot of *that* kind of riff-raff living here." There is nothing sadder than hearing the word "that" in reference to people. Her "good Lord" would love everyone. Why can't *she*?

Even the woman who rented me my bike said, "We don't really have minorities here. We are still pretty pristine."

Pristine? As in fresh and green and new? I had to work really hard to keep a lid on it. I needed that bike!

I needed that bike to get away from people.

I needed that bike so I could ride *through* towns with population signs that read 600. Which sounds charming. Until you are there.

I needed that bike to forget the bigotry of some people, not to mention my own failings.

I needed that bike in order to get lost. Just me and my own long thoughts.

By day three, after passing so many lakes, I started to think a lot about the difference between lake country and coastal shores.

Lakes, I was beginning to see, are more reflective of a way of life where people know, or want to know, what's on the other side.

But a shoreline, well, you never know. Everything is fluid. My neighbors in Seattle are a rainbow of color coming from every corner of the globe. I felt such a wave of homesickness, I had to stop pedaling and pull over.

I happily arrived at my train car.

No bears. No wolves. No perverts.

I felt more confident giving that reading than I have ever felt in my life.

A Peek Inside

I am always telling book clubs that I love reading for them; that they chose *my* book feels like a great compliment.

But I don't really mean it.

Well, not the compliment part, I do mean that. It's the best feeling to have readers. Without readers, I'd be like a balloon with a long-drawn-out leak. It's just that when I visit a club, any club, I can end up feeling like I am on the outside looking in.

Last night I read for such a club. The women go way back with each other. And when I say way back, I mean *all* the way back. To grade school. It wasn't that they didn't help me feel welcome, they did. But their closeness got me to thinking a lot about transience on my drive back to the city. A sense of dislocation started to creep in. My sense of place, or lack of it, was made even more clear: no matter how many years I live in the Northwest, I will never be *of* it. Not in the way they are.

Right out of college I went looking for something else, soared off to the West Coast to find it, and never turned back. Traveling taught me so much about myself. I left my parents, my siblings, my first friends, and never had second thoughts. I didn't hold on to one friend from grade school. Which ultimately makes me more of a transient—on the surface, anyway, doesn't it? To my family, I am like a bird, flying here, there, and everywhere.

It's a long drive from Bothell. So I started to think more about family. How some of us settle where they are. And others where they are *not*.

I am afraid I fall deeply into the second category.

Consequently, I have sort of grown without roots. Like fern moss.

But even if I don't have family close by to turn to, the people I have learned to trust have become like family. They accept me as I am. It matters little that we come from different countries and cultures that test our communication skills. And this goes way beyond the difficult pronunciation of each other's names (a steep learning curve for all of us), we look in on each other's pets and plants and children. We gather up the mail. We keep good track of each other.

The most unexpected outcome is that they have taught me how to stay true to myself. Truer than I've been around real family. *You are such a coward for saying that. It's not how you really feel,* is how I felt after so many conversations with my mother, my father, my uncles and aunts. I needed to lie to them; pretend. Ask me why this is, and I will likely want to vent. Or cry.

And I thought that I'd come to fully accept this less family/more friends way of life, but it is never that simple.

The first time I saw the Olympic Mountains rising out of the clouds, I felt a sense of belonging so strong

I wouldn't let anyone talk me into coming home. I thought, *what are you talking about? I am home.* This is why it's difficult to put a name to what I started to feel in the driveway in Bothell, even before I put my key in the ignition.

It isn't only the book club. Fall always does this to me. I should be used to it, accustomed to how it feels to have a recurring homing impairment. Half of the reason is due to the fact that we live in a free culture, blessed with a dizzying array of choices that can stir the reality of where I live with all the possibilities of where I *could* live, possibly, maybe, perhaps . . .

The other half is part of a larger story. My family had to leave home in order to move forward. They stuck their necks out. I think this is why I continue to visit such tight-knit clubs of wine-sipping strangers. They help me stick *my* neck out. Maybe not as far as my parents did, but it's risky putting yourself out there.

But it's a peek inside, too, like glimpsing where all of your decisions, good and bad, have settled. And how well they have.

Blink

I HAVE THIS FRIEND WHO is going through a rough time.

And it's the worst thing to be sad around the holidays. You hear a carol and everything inside you recoils, like feeling cold and warm at the same time.

Before her husband died, I went to visit. "Open the wine," she yelled from upstairs, "I'll be right down." I found the wine amid so many prescription bottles all I could think was, *it won't be long.*

It wasn't. Two months later, I was at his memorial service.

Now, I am a little embarrassed to admit this, but I remember sitting there trying to remember if they ever got along. Because they fought. They fought all the time. When she described one argument to me, she was so upset her hands trembled. And I said something like, "couples argue, it's no big deal." But that was early on, when I still hoped that the two of them would make it.

Before I started to worry that they *would*.

When she announced her engagement, I did not call back right away. I have a little problem faking enthusiasm.

Because he did not just argue with her, he made everyone feel uncomfortable, that is just the sort of man he was. He seemed to enjoy embarrassing my friend in front of *her* friends, as if he would stow his criticisms until we were all together and then, one by one, fling them at her. What is more, I think he wanted to fling them at her in front of us, it's why he would tag along in the first place. Then, once everyone was looking at him, mortified, he would act like he could not figure out what horrible thing he had done.

Even so, after he died, all I had to do was look in her eyes to see how desperate she felt, reminding me how alone we can feel after a loss, any loss. That we continue to love someone who has hurt us was not news to me. "Do you think I'll ever find another man like him?" she said.

Why would you want to? I thought, but of course I didn't say that. I know the simplest way to show support is to never come up dry in the optimism department. "Of course you will!" I said.

"It's just that I hate being alone."

"We're all alone in the end," I answered, not quite believing I did so with such a tired saying. It's just that I did not, *do* not, want her to settle for another man who makes her feel bad about herself. And I could just kick myself for bringing up the presidential debates after promising myself that I wouldn't because my friend is much more conservative than I am. But I was working so hard at not bringing them up, I brought them up.

"You know," she said, "Trump is just what this country needs."

I blinked. I smiled, blinked again, harder this time, but I was not all that surprised by her comment, not really. When it comes to politics, my friend is always saying things that sound crazy to me. But that is not the point.

The point is that no two people can ever be on the same page about everything. If we are, I am pretty sure one of us is lying. And the whole point is to *accept* each other's differences.

Besides, I knew what my friend was really saying: A man like Trump may be just what *she* needs. I mean, she settled for money before. And she knew I knew because she started to chuckle. Next, because the line between emotions is impossibly thin, she fell apart.

I think an even truer thing I needed to learn about friendship began right then, after she said another thing I don't believe for a second is true: "We had a good marriage," and this time I didn't blink.

THE SWEETER MIDDLE

"LISTEN," MY NEIGHBOR Margie said last month when we were sitting around in her living room, all very merry on eggnog she swore she hardly spiked. "What you and Larry have is rare." I believe the next words she used were "freaking rare" which is about as racy as Margie ever speaks. She was touching my arm now, "I mean, you still hold *hands*."

"Not always," I said. Because her comment made me remember a not-so-handholding moment earlier. Sure, Larry and I walked hand in hand up to her building, but on the walk over he got so mad at me he yanked his hand away. All because I asked him (for the hundredth time) if he had remembered to send a gift to his sister, Caren.

"You *know*," he said, in the drawn-out way he uses when he's pretending something he is about to say is all very spontaneous, but it is not, he has actually used the same excuse many times before, "you are so much better at choosing gifts."

"You mean like when you say I'm better at washing dishes because you don't want to stop watching soccer?"

"You mean like when *you* say I'm better at changing the oil."

This is what Larry does when he is trying to lead us away from the edge and feeling his way toward the sweeter middle. And because he eventually loses his anger (generally by the next day), I reached for his hand again. But instead of just admitting that he had forgotten to send the gift, he just shrugged.

"Why can't you just admit that you forgot?" I said. "What's the big deal?"

This question always rankles him. He yanks his hand away for the second time.

I believe I could string our marriage together with these little yanks of the flesh and what it takes to come around to holding on to each other again.

Actually, I think I can string most of my life together by remembering one little yank of the heartstrings or another that seems to pop up out of nowhere and take me by surprise.

Like the other day at Goodwill. I went to look for a gift for Margie's gift exchange (she asked that all of the gifts be second hand), and I saw a salad plate that belonged to my mother's pattern. It's not a rare pattern, I think the A & P used to give them away if you spent enough. I never dreamed the pattern would mean so much to me down the line. Or that now, whenever I see a white plate stamped in the middle with golden wheat stalks, so much emotion would come sweeping back until my heart either melts or freezes. Depending.

Depending on whether, in the here and now, I can handle it—the confusing intricacies of my mother's love, my love, *our* love.

Depending on whether I remember that there is no perfect mother, no perfect daughter, no perfect way to give love. Or to receive it.

Depending on whether I take the time to remind myself (again) that love is in the moment. And there is no perfect moment, either. And if I don't accept *that*, I will harden into some ridiculous expectation of love.

I buy the plate.

I do not know if Larry and I are really all that rare, I know plenty of great couples.

I do know that what we share feels true, but only because we work hard to keep it that way. And sometimes, *stressful* times, it feels as if there is hardly enough time to figure out what we are really quarreling about, let alone resolve it, before another tiff pops up. And that the only secret, if there has to be a secret—Margie says there has to be a secret—is that one of us needs to find the humor in it, and fast. Or you can bet one of us is going to yank our hand away, and I would rather do anything than walk up to a friend's door two paces ahead or behind, holding on to nothing but pride.

CLOSE

YEARS AGO, I DID A LOT of research for a book I was writing about friendship. I wrote down things in a tiny notebook, things like: "You don't need a thick skin to have friends. You need a porous one."

And there was a moment last night when I was about to share this quote with the audience of the Unitarian Women's Retreat just as one woman piped up to say that according to an article she'd read, as many as twenty percent of American adults do not have a single close friend, and we took a detour. "This means," she said, whipping out her phone to do the math, except she could not figure how to use her calculator. "Anyway," she said, still fumbling with her phone, "a *lot* of people are friendless."

Another woman said, "I heard that people are turning to Siri for contact, but that's not contact. Why would I care if a phone knows I'm lonely?"

The question went around the room: What do we mean by a *close* friend?

"Someone who will offer to pick me up at the airport," one said.

"Someone who will sit with you after your mother dies and let you cry for hours," said another, "that's close enough for me."

"I called my friend Lynette when my pressure cooker exploded," I said. "Split pea soup was everywhere. I needed someone who would calm me down *and* pick up a sponge."

"Frankly, I don't have a friend who would clean up split pea soup," another said. "Close, but not *that* close."

I had to think. Let's see, I have at least three friends I can call when a crisis strikes. And a more recent one that I hope will be as long-lasting. But I've learned that the closer a friendship is, the more fragile it can become. And if it comes apart, it is hard to trust the earth under your feet. Which reminds me of another truth I wrote in my notebook, "tread carefully."

The youngest woman in the group said she found it difficult to keep friends, that she tends to wind up disappointed. And because so many other women at so many other Q & A's have expressed the same problem, I assumed, wrongly, that she was struggling with friendship because of an unrealistic perfection quest. I was about to say that even in my closest friendships there has been at least one moment when we could have parted ways, and how I could have saved myself a lot of pain if I'd just brought my expectations down a notch or two. I nearly shared another quote: "Friendships are like marriages. We love each other, yes, but we also need to be able to dislike each other sometimes. And be bored by each other." Luckily, before I said any of this, I asked, "What do you mean by disappointed?"

She stared at me.

"What disappoints you the most?" I repeated.

And this was her unabashed and totally unexpected reply: "You mean, like, when she slept with my *husband*?"

There was a silence.

And then there was laughing. Laughing, laughing, and more laughing. It still brings a smile to my face— her response. It was so unassertive, yet so real. Even her puzzlement had a funny effect. The whole evening was special like that.

I think this is what people have always meant about being in the moment. That no matter how well I plan ahead—going over my notes, knowing my material—it is usually something totally unexpected that makes everything work, and writing about it is like having those moments back.

And I want them back.

LUCKY CHARM

THE BEAUTY OF A LUCKY CHARM is that it does not have to make sense to anyone else, it is a personal attachment. Mine include a paperweight globe, shells, and a stone with the word INSPIRE inscribed on it.

The globe is a reminder to keep things in perspective. The shells recall the year I taught dance throughout the Caribbean and how afraid I was at times. "You pay closer attention when you are afraid," they remind me. The stone is a gift from a young friend, Rose, who said one of my columns inspired her.

"Really?" I said, because I remember wondering if younger women would object to what I had to say. It's why the stone reminds me that every time I sit down to write, fear is a huge part of it.

In the piece, I say that satisfying work is the most gratifying part of life. And this is what I was afraid of. It sounded like the kind of thing a woman who had put profession first would say.

Which is what it was.

It would have been safer to say that work is second to love, family, faith, the kind of thing people say all the time whether they mean it or not. I also said it was okay to inch along until you find the work you really want to do, even if it scares you to death.

"But *that* won't pay the bills," you may be thinking.

But see, I have come to believe that money is over-rated. Too little is horrible, no one wants too little. But less is not the end of the world. I don't know how much of this awareness comes from being a writer or a dancer, or both, but I can't stop trying to figure out the conflict between what we really want in life and what we are told we *should* want. And why "should" so often wins out.

Also, I said that if we have the courage to do what we love, it is our best career choice. But in order to *continue*, most of us cannot fall prey to owning all the new and expensive things people buy to try and ensure happiness.

After college, I worked as a waitress. One restaurant after another until I threw a drink at a famous patron who said a very inappropriate thing with his hand on my behind.

I am glad I was fired. Because the money was good. Better than good. I might have stayed on too long because of that, and not got on with my dream of opening a dance studio.

Well, obviously dance studios do not pay all that well. So I left the city and found an affordable town to move to, and a dirt-cheap barn to rent with a solid wood floor.Heaven to a dancer.

My life moved on. And so did Rose's.

Rose went to work for the huge, thrusting, tech world. The last time I heard from her she gave reasons why she had no time to write. I have often wondered what would have happened if she had allowed herself to keep at it, without mortgaging a condo on Capitol Hill, and buying all the stylish furnishings to fill it.

I know how difficult it can be to choose enthusiasm over a lofty paycheck. I also know how many well-paid professionals I meet who cannot remember the last time they felt excited about their work, who speak as if they are simply putting in the hours.

Recently in a gift store on Bainbridge Island, I came across a display of small stones like mine. Their engravings read: SMART. PROUD. POWERFUL. And I was thrilled to find two new ones: PERSISTENCE. PERSEVERANCE.

My favorite inscription used to be INSPIRE.

And I am happy I inspired you, Rose.

But it is only the first step.

FAILINGS

This morning, early, I poked my nose out the window and I knew I had to go for a bike ride; that sitting at my desk, which is pretty much how I always begin my day, just wouldn't do.

Of course, the whole truth is that I do not know what to do with myself after I finish a book. As I say this (both wishing that I wasn't here again and relieved that I am), I know that with all the extra time on my hands, combined with the fact that bike riding makes me feel happier than just about any other physical activity, I have two choices: Begin yet another book. Or be more physically active.

And since I enjoy being physically engaged in getting from here to there as much as being mentally engaged in getting from here to there, I will choose the former.

Because I need a little down time.

Because converting my thoughts to intelligible words has a limit, and it is not always the sky.

Because sometimes I need movement, not stillness.

The next minute my hands are slipping on my sneakers so fast I dropped one of them twice.

The thing I love most about riding is that I see more, and this morning, the newest jury-rigged tarp strung between branches along the waterfront bikeway is hard to miss. I find everything about makeshift survival depressing and admirable at the same time.

I slowed.

A young man is standing on a sheet of muddy cardboard next to his tarp and I have this clear impression of something tender and good and yet countless kinds of wrong. He (father or brother, I don't know) is holding a baby girl, maybe a year old. Their campsite is pretty tidy, but the one next to them reeks of the worst smells. He is battling some kind of addiction; all you have to do is look at him to see someone struggling to cope and losing the struggle. I rode off wondering how long before we will not even find homelessness worth a second look because it's so common.

I have friends who lean both ways.

One thinks that the homeless should be "rounded up." That is exactly what she said. Like the sunspot she had lasered off her arm, we should simply remove them.

Another started volunteering at a women's shelter.

My mother used to say: *There but for the grace of God, go I.*

I say: God grant me the serenity to accept the things I cannot change, courage to change the things I can, and the patience *not* to smack the head of the man in my building who said, "Mary Lou, Mary *Lou*," repeating my name twice so that I, silly woman, would see the world as he does if I know what is good for me. "What's the point of bike lanes if they encourage more people who can't afford cars?"

"You are an imbecile," I said.

It is the kind of thing I say when I am fed up.

It is the kind of thing I say when I feel desperate about our failings.

I tell you, homeless people, homeless *children*, are our truest failing. If someone had said to me ten years ago that this is what our city would look like today, I would not have believed them.

GUIDANCE

I WAS STANDING IN LINE at the movies. It was a particularly long line, so I was happy just to settle into people-watching. Until the woman behind me answered her phone.

And, like *that*, my usual way of tuning out cell chatter was no longer possible. "Stop calling me," she softly yelled. "I'm taking the day off." After a pause, "Not from work, from *you!*"

Yes, I eavesdrop.

No, I do not always share what I hear.

But there was something about this conversation that was so obviously why I have two ears and one laptop.

"You're doing it again," and from the tone of her voice whoever was on the other end was annoying her and has done so a lot. "You don't *listen.*"

Naturally, I assumed she was talking to the man in her life. But to be fair, it could also be her wife, mother, father, a sibling, a friend.

Though likely not a younger friend.

Only someone old enough to know how limited time can feel, so that they are more likely to forgive and forget could weather such a conversation. But even then, it's dicey. (And why we more easily forgive others, even those less deserving than ourselves, is beyond me.)

"No you *don't*. You go into sports mode. Defense, defense, defense. You do not want to *have* a conversation. You want to *win* the conversation."

Ah. The man, then.

This sports analogy might not apply to your husband or partner. But in my circles, women talk about it all the time, how rare good listening skills are. My friend Stephanie says good kissing is one thing, but if her date asks a question and then listens closely to her reply, now *that* she finds sexy.

I wanted to turn around and give this woman a thumbs up. But there are times when you know it is inappropriate to offer advice or even encouragement, and this felt like one of those times. Also, I was afraid she would hang up.

But doesn't everyone need encouragement? When I have a really rotten day, there is no better friend in the world than someone who has been there. Who knows.

I even thought of something funny to say, a line I remembered from *Roseanne*. After Jackie commented how patient Dan was, Roseanne said, "Yeah, Jackie, but he didn't come out of the box that way. I've spent years training him. *Years!*"

Although I knew what I was really doing. My mind was already writing the story. This is what it's like. I can't turn it off even if I want to. And why I love it when I find myself standing in the right place at the right time.

Listening (nosiness, whatever you want to call it) can lead me right into the crux of what others are struggling with, and I want to know what others are struggling with. I like hearing people say aloud something that may have been eating at them for a long time. I don't want to shy away from it.

Whatever *it* is.

Hmmm. I am pretty sure it is guidance.

But guidance *alone* isn't the whole of it. Guidance is only the beginning.

The full circle is that when we listen to the people around us, it can feel as though we are being guided together. Mutually. That's the effect it has on me.

And this is how I learn best. By mutual effect.

The Gamble

Recently I was going through a file of old articles and I found a cover story I wrote for the Seattle *Post-Intelligencer*, illustrated by a drawing of a woman (meant to be me) sitting in a fifth-floor window, holding on to a stem that is reaching for the sidewalk. At the end of the stem is a dangling root. Clearly, I was still trying to find my place in Seattle and all that showed in the artist's sketch.

Rereading the article reminded me of what a gamble it felt like to find myself living in the city again after so many years in Port Townsend. For the first few years, I was just so alive, professional opportunities were everywhere.

At the same time, reality took on a somewhat disorienting version of its previous self.

That is the image that comes to me now as I sit here remembering how the same sense of disorientation struck hard (*hard*, I tell you) this past weekend. Out of nowhere, like a genie from a lamp, just when I needed to feel otherwise.

A woman who heard me speak in Seattle was determined to create an event in Eugene, Oregon "with you as our speaker," she said, shaking my hand so eagerly there was an awkward moment over whether we should just keep shaking hands, or hug, or cheek kiss. Everything about her was like this, very can-do, so I pretty much knew she would follow through.

She did. Eighty women came to her fundraising tea.

I am lucky for the invitations I receive.

But luck is luck. And it can change in an instant.

I received an email. Since I was coming to Eugene, would I pay a visit to a book club in the area, as well?

Oh lord.

The hostess picked me up downtown. We drove up into the hills, and as soon as a private gate swung open, I started to feel uncomfortable. But once the bear skin (hung over two massive front doors) came into focus, the whole course of the evening began to shift without my really knowing how to steady it.

Situations do not go wrong all at once. There is one thing, and then there is another thing. And in this case the bear skin was the first thing.

Now, the first thing makes you wonder if you are in the wrong place with the wrong people until your insides whisper: *Ut oh.*

The second thing can make your *ut oh* turn into *help! Will someone please help me?*

There is brutality in the world at every turn, I know this. I am no Pollyanna.

Well, actually that is not true. I am sort of a Pollyanna.

So when the stark reality of trophy killing becomes the reality I am forced to deal with, I suddenly grasp the third thing: that I will have to find a way to cope with a collection of severed heads hung over the fireplace.

Severed heads! Hung over the fireplace!

Wildebeest, Zebra, Rhinoceros, Cheetah—horned, hairy, magnificent, *endangered*. They glared at me. They broke my heart. They cried *this is where some people believe we belong. And that shooting us, even from an airplane, is their right.*

The hostess told me they were from Africa. She seemed to think this mattered and that I would be impressed. I wondered why she had not thought that I, a writer, might be appalled. I know this sounds like a stereotype, but in my case, I do not even have words for how much the stereotype *fits*.

I thought: *After reading my book you said you felt like you knew me. My god, why?* My sentiments shine through in pretty much everything I write. I must have said something that would indicate to a reader that I am opposed to cold-blooded killing of innocent animals, right?

Honestly, I cannot remember. People think I remember everything I write. In truth, I have written so much over the years that as soon as I stand, the words run off. I am a blank slate again.

The wine started to flow, as it generally does, in vast amounts. And when the hostess handed me a glass, I took it, but I did not take a sip.

Not one sip.

An outsider is a dangerous thing to be without total sobriety.

I tried to project confidence. I said, "Turn off your phones, please," as if it was a logical request. It was not a logical request. It was an order. I did not want to end up on someone's Facebook page sitting anywhere near those awful heads.

I read a few pages from my book, talked some.

A hand flies up. "Where do you get your inspiration?"

The dreaded question. Only because I can never simplify the answer enough, even if I knew where on earth to begin. I do not wait for inspiration. I go to work every day whether I am inspired or not. A lot of mornings I find myself doing all kinds of things to avoid my office, my desk, my mind.

Instead of sidestepping the issue of politics, as I usually do, I said—and I knew I was setting myself up, but I didn't care—"Hillary Clinton inspires me. I admire women who dedicate their lives to shattering the glass ceiling."

The hostess cleared her throat.

Someone immediately brought up Hillary's "lie."

Benghazi? Again? You have got to be kidding me. There is war on so many fronts, refugees fleeing from so many countries, and this is what you fixate on? What is it with Benghazi? What is it? What is it? What is it? Why this lie (if it was, in fact, a lie, which investigations on both sides have proved it was not), and conveniently forget "weapons of mass destruction," a lie that arrived us into this abyss of terror that the entire world has fallen into. But what I really wanted to ask is *why are you so hard on her? Because she is a woman? Just like you. What are you so afraid of?*

I said, "She's been an activist since college, the First Lady, Secretary of State. How much harder does a woman have to work at something to prove she's capable of the job?" Maybe it was the beady eyes of the Jackal that forced me to speak up, but I could not wait to get back down to the flats by the railroad tracks to my small inn. Just to *be* there. Happily alone.

I sent for an Uber.

There were fifteen women present. I sold only two books to the same woman who did not for a second look like she intended to read it. I think she felt sorry for me.

That's how it goes. Some readings are a total flop. It's all part of the gamble.

And while flops can be wounding to the ego, they are (ahem, in hindsight) just as often reassuring.

Actually, they are better than reassuring.

Like trees growing through the sidewalk, flops teach us how to withstand.

And that, I believe, makes them better (again, in *hindsight*) than just about anything.

Contrasts

This is a story about contrasts.

And Seattle is a red-hot center of contrasts lately.

It's also a story about courage that belongs to a woman from Vietnam.

Though a smidgen of the courage belongs to me, too, because this is another immigration story, and I'm determined to tell it.

Even if at the end of the story, I just shake my head.

I love a good pampering, who doesn't?

So yesterday, I took full advantage of my husband's generosity: a surprise mani/pedi at a downtown spa.

The last time I had a mani/pedi was when my mother was dying. I was also writing a book that maybe I should have put away but writing kept me sane through all that. When the giver of *that* mani/pedi asked, "How you?" I burst into tears. I felt so vulnerable, I cried about everything. She swept me into the back room and dug her thumbs into my shoulders. "Dollar a minute," she said. I asked for an hour. Half per shoulder. She set the timer.

This time, a woman named Phuong inspects my nails, and she smiles as though she is *delighted* to inspect my nails. I thought of what my friend James said about perpetually smiling people, "Some of the least-happy people you ever want to meet." Except I did not get the feeling Phuong is unhappy. "You look so cheerful," I say.

"I love it here, that's why," she says, smiling, smiling.

There are four other women getting "treatments." I wondered if I was the only one who felt caught between a deep deserving calm and tinges of guilt since I find it improbable to "love" massaging a stranger's hands and feet.

I also couldn't help but wonder, *who are these women who rub our hands and feet and what are their stories?* Because a genuinely smiling person extending genuine kindness is a rare occurrence these days. Our city is changing so quickly that trendy, copy-cat behavior is everywhere. But genuine kindness, not so much.

Take the echoed, "it's all good." Even my elderly neighbor said it when I thanked him for holding the elevator. I never understood why "you're welcome" became dated, and I was just getting used to "of course," pleased that "no problem" is finally seen as the snub it can feel like. But nothing is ever "all good" for anyone, ever. Why say that it is?

"What brought you to Seattle?" I ask Phuong.

"The internet," she said. "I reply to my husband."

Oh no. Mail order bride. It's always been like this. And because she is all of twenty, I say, "Please do not tell me he is eighty years old."

She looked at me and blinked before answering, "He good to me. He not kidnap me. He not Chinese."

I did not know if she would want to talk about any of this, but I had read that China's one-child policy was recently abolished after it led a whole generation to abort female fetuses. The country now has at least 24 million "surplus" men ages 20 to 45.

But she was happy to tell me more. She said that because there are not enough women to marry in China, the men sneak over the border to kidnap girls from her village. "My cousin was stolen from our playground. We learn enough Chinese and English so we can get home if we are kidnapped."

"That is just so awful," I said, queasy all of a sudden.

"More awful when they take only our kidneys."

That, I remember, was a crystallizing moment for me.

Here is where my story is all about courage: I do not think people like Phuong share such stories to entertain us, or shock us, but because they need to talk about what they've gone through to stay alive. And it is amazing to me that considering what she'd just told me, she managed to give the impression that she is entirely appreciative of the opportunities she's been given.

And here is the contrast: the woman sitting directly next to me never looked up from her phone to acknowledge Phuong, or the story she'd just had the privilege to hear, other than to ask if the overhead light could be turned up. And when she was reminded that phones were not allowed, she repeated another echo I find disingenuous, "whatever."

I thought, *would it kill you to be present*? When I asked about the logo on her tote bag, she said that it was *not* a logo, but a brand (duh), and that the rest of her "team-builders" were in the sauna.

This is the part where I shake my head.

By the time I get to the dressing room, it looks as though the team builders had been carrying on like a frat party. What a mess.

It is so easy to forget someone always has to clean up the mess.

My friend Marlin was a cleaning lady when she first came to this country. To help pay for college, *I* was a cleaning lady. The stories we can tell.

I pick up the wet towels and throw them in the basket.

SAVED

IN A RECENT COLUMN I SHARED how when my mother was dying, "writing saved me."

It prompted a reader named Kristen to contact me to say that writing was the only thing saving her, too, hiding nothing about her despair in a funny email that took some of the heartache out of the situation both for herself and for me.

Kristen, thank you. In times like this, when we wonder if we can get through it, laughter lifts the weight right out. I know because I am the same way.

But to be honest, writing was not the *only* thing that saved me.

And if there is any doubt about how restorative the sea can be, this story attests to it.

When I first visited the island of Oahu, I would never have dreamed that I would wind up swimming out to the reef. I hugged the shoreline, afraid to venture out.

My world had grown small by then, the way it does when someone you love is failing. My makeshift desk, my mother's bedside, to the beach and back, that was my day. There was not much I could do for my mother other than to be there. I longed to talk to her, but she could no longer speak. I longed even for the sound of her constant complaining, but she could not wake. I stared at her unresponsive face. Oh, the expressions she used to make. The looks she could give.

When we are young, we take so much about our parents' features for granted. I know I did. Eyes, ears, nose, mouth, chin. Like most kids, I assumed that they would always be active, *working*. I never thought about how terrible it would be to lose them.

And it was terrible. It was so terrible.

I used to ride my bike from the hospice home to Kaimana Beach, a mile east of Waikiki. It was there I first watched a man the locals lovingly call "Big Brian" swim out past the reef.

You would not know Big Brian was a serious swimmer to look at him, he is paunchy for an athlete. He does not do a series of stretches before he dives in. He stands with his feet in the water and talks to other swimmers and listening to him was the beginning of my swimming education. I learned to call the fluttering cone at the end of the channel a windsock not a flag, and to never get in a swimmer's way once they hit the water or I'd have to endure a local stink eye. Really, I never knew how nuanced a look could *be* until I swam with Polynesians.

The first time I struck up a conversation with Big Brian he told me that if I stopped swimming "like a chicken," I'd eventually "be lucky enough" to swim over a *manō*. Just the way he said it, I knew he meant a shark. I did not feel it was my place to say, "Please do not tell me that."

One day a woman named Deb swam up beside me and said she would swim to the windsock if I did.

That worked.

From then on, I knew that swimming toward the horizon offered something so unlike "chicken" swimming, so much more.

By then, the ocean provided the high point of my day the way a steady, supportive friend is there for you. And swimming filled in the lows. I have a clearer sense of this now.

Big Brian mentioned other creatures I would see, too, and he was right. A few days later, I bumped into a turtle. We just did not *see* each other. The experience changed the way I thought about the ocean and myself within it, as if *my* shell had been struck, and a huge part of my fear fell off.

The Green Sea Turtle, known as "Honu," symbolizes good luck to the Hawaiian people. And, according to one of my mother's nurses, shows up as your guardian spirit. It took no effort to convince myself. I had needed a guardian spirit ever since landing at the airport.

The same feeling came over me when I was surprised by the heft of a monk seal and startled by a Moray Eel (I personally do not care for Moray Eels). My first instinct was to bolt, but I swam closer as it pulled back inside the reef. I pictured it down there saying to another eel, "just another crazy *haole*."

And I was crazy. A little. One day in the water, I had this wild vision of myself as a papaya. As if my skin had to come open to be fully appreciated, and I had not come open yet. I was too busy holding myself together.

Still, no shark.

Until my return to the island months later to face the awful, gut-wrenching week of cleaning-out-your-mom's-belongings, when more than once I did come open. Actually, I went a little ballistic. "I can't do this!" I screamed.

But, of course, I could.

Swimming felt like the only effort I could pull off with any grace. I even gathered my courage and swam *the* brag-able swim of Kaimana Beach, from the windsock to the pink Royal Hawaiian Hotel. Except I swam from the hotel to the windsock, against the current. I remember thinking it was a good metaphor for the rest of my life.

And there it was. A reef shark was lodged between two shelves of coral, as if resting. Seeing it tied my respect for sharks to my overwhelming fear of finding one. And though a creature that can kill you never looks quite as terrifying below the waterline as it does above, I swam away.

Boy, did I.

And every day since, I feel as though I finally understand what it means to call oneself an ocean swimmer.

"Hey, Brian! I saw a shark!"

"Yeah. How big?"

"Too big," I said.

"Whitetip," he said, but my story excited the casual look in his eyes, not that he'd ever say so, "the little guy." This was Brian's way of telling me that there would always be bigger challenges ahead if I kept swimming.

And there have been.

More and more of them, more and more often.

Even now, when I feel as though I cannot see my future clearly, the sea is transparent. Above, below, and on either side, the world opens.

On shore, the door into clarity rarely opens as wide as I'd like. Even if I have no intention of going back, I often can't see forward. The feeling is like being stranded somewhere unfamiliar at midnight with no ride home. It's why when I say that I am "going swimming," I am sort of pretending.

Because, really, I am saving myself.

Here is where I will briefly mention how it feels to see your first Tiger shark. Yes, its stripes are visible, and, yes, it is terrifying.

So terrifying, that all I could think was *it is a mistake, all this swimming.*

And the next day I went swimming.

An Enviable Couple

I MET S., WHO IS RESPONSIBLE for making me laugh more than any other friend, in my dance class. I loved this young student with an old soul. We became friends. We have had lots and lots of fun over the years.

Naturally, there have been tears, too. She cries easily and so do I. But our tears are so unlike what most people think of when they think of tears. We consider ours a rite, as important as talking.

Still, I am older than S. by twenty years. Which makes for tears she has not even begun to cry yet. And when her marriage expectations skitter off into fantasyland, a part of me feels it's my duty to guide her gently back to reality, while the other part knows to just listen; to silently accept where we are, independently, at this moment in time.

The alternative is that I become her mother. But she has a mother. I am her friend. Even when I do not feel like her friend because I feel like her mother.

Either way, there is no gentle way of saying, "You can't even *hope* that he'll know how you feel if you don't tell him. And yes you *will* have to slowly explain the complexities of a woman's emotions again and again with no guarantee that he will understand what on *earth* you are talking about (especially when you say you can be happy and sad at the same time), remember a word of it, or not be bored out of his skull. And if he closes his eyes, no, he is not still listening. He is asleep.

The writer Phyllis Miletich was one of my older friends. I am sure I made Phyllis laugh in the way people laugh when what they really want to do is roll their eyes. She gave me great advice: "Don't try to make your husband your girlfriend. You have girlfriends for that."

When I shared this advice with S., I saw the look in her eyes. I have seen this look before. It says, "But I *want* him to be my best friend!" And I think to myself, *well, that is what every woman wants. Until she knows better.*

S. is balancing a lot: a toddler, a husband, a career. And she is struggling. She has struggled before. But nothing like this. Last time we met, she mentioned marriage counseling.

I did not know what to say. My thoughts on the subject felt too wide to sum up on a narrow barstool. I could not say then what I have sat down to write now, which is that the most enviable marriage I have ever witnessed was between two crows. How many couples take the time to do nothing but that daily round-dance in the nest to smooth out the kinks? *You do not need a marriage counselor, just watch the crows.*

But on that day, I could not say this to S., she was too upset.

I could only take a sip of my Syrah and *wish* that I could.

It was my second glass, but it wasn't second-glass wisdom when I finally found the nerve to say, "I watched a female crow let the male bring food to the nest and then she squawked until he left. He seemed to accept, without question or objection, that she just could not deal with hatchlings and him at the same time. Now tell me, how many men do you know like this?"

A look passed between us. We started to laugh.

In mind, I was already preparing the email I would write to S. that night because I always have this rush of emotion right after I see someone I love. As soon as I am safely at home, I want to reach out again. This time I wanted to say that it doesn't matter how passionate things are in the beginning—so sweet that you reject all of your fears and believe that this time things will be different—he will *still* make you crazy sometimes.

Bonkers, total meltdown crazy.

And he will still make you cry. Often. Mainly around the full moon.

But so will your friends, siblings, parents, especially your mom. Which is so unfair to our gender it makes the air around me go still.

Actually, I think anyone you genuinely love will make you cry eventually if they haven't already.

Luckily, most misunderstandings can be forgiven if we take the time to talk. But even if we do find the time, mending is a lot of work. I've found it gets easier once we figure out who we flat-out love from who we want to love, or think we *should* love, except every time we find ourselves in their company, we get this bristly feeling, and we know not to get drunk because we may just act out and say the one thing we've been holding onto like a dog with a chew toy. Or we do get drunk and say something mean on purpose because we need to find a way to let go of the relationship. And ninety-nine percent of the time, alcohol will complete this for us. It's why we ordered a martini in the first place.

So that is the email I wrote.

Pretty much.

I cut some of it short before I swung my legs over the side of my chair, eager for bed. I had only just pressed SEND, and already I felt as though I had found the best way to help my friend.

I snuggled up under the covers with my husband of four decades, a man I love so deeply I can still feel satisfied by something as small as the way he clicks his pen when he talks on the phone and I think, *remember those clicks, Mary Lou, that you just had the privilege of hearing them.*

And yet, and *yet* . . . there are other times when those clicks will scrape my last nerve and I will squawk at him until privilege does not matter anymore, I am so *over* those clicks.

All This

Here I am again, walking away from the podium after giving what I believe to be a pretty good presentation. I did not flinch, even once, when a woman seated at the nearest round table kept nodding.

Generally I like nods. They prove that someone is actually listening. Except this nodder wore floppy metal earrings that jingled, key-like, every time she moved her head. It was like listening to a custodian dance through the room.

It has taken me years to not react to all the surprises I am faced with on the spot.

Though I can still have my moments.

And they can still turn my cheeks two shades of red.

Especially when I say something I perhaps should have kept to myself. Like when I was asked what the most difficult part of speaking is, I said, while looking directly at the woman nodding, that jewelry can pose a problem.

No one seemed to get the joke.

To save myself, I said, "But *no* jingle compares to eating sounds," trying to make it sound as if that is what I meant all along. I was referring to the man who sat in the front row at the Wallingford library munching corn nuts, a sound that has come to represent all the other sounds I have learned to cope with while staying on point.

Next, I admitted that while luncheon speaking (and in my world this means trying to keep people's attention while they pass bread baskets, kvetch about how cold the soup is, and eye the desert trays from across the room) has its own set of challenges, nothing is worse than unkindness. And how I have learned to be wary of people who walk up to my book table with an expression that is maybe not hostile, but it is definitely not kind, either.

I knew right off that I would have to give details, so I explained how the look on one woman's face would seem perfectly normal had I just addressed, say, terrorism, or the Alaska Way Viaduct. But my talk was about supporting each other. As I watched her approach, I could not help but think, *I've triggered something. There is scorn in her eyes.* "And really, who doesn't enjoy a scornful look now and again."

This made everyone chuckle.

It is always best when they do that.

I shared the rest of the story, too, how, as soon as the woman reached my table, she said, "that was cute," without smiling. I felt a slow hiss seep out of the pride I felt. "Cute" was not at all what I was going for.

"So, where do you see yourself going with all this?" the woman continued.

"All this?" I said.

"Where do you see yourself in five years?"

I have limited tolerance for timeline questions. I never know if it is a need to instruct or to compete, but the two seem to mix in people like this. They cannot seem to fathom that life can be more entrepreneurial than they know it to be. "It doesn't matter," I said, and after a deep breath, "because there is no brass ring in five years because there is no brass ring. I have to be fully in the moment to be effective," words that came to me because of good advice I'd received from a colleague: "If you think everyone in the audience is going to be kind, you really need to consider doing something else," she said. "But if you stick with it, it is good to have a few good comebacks up your sleeve. Memorize them. There is nothing more difficult than preserving your dignity when you are taken aback."

I could see the woman's mind working, wondering what to say next. But she just stared at me like I was clueless and walked away.

I told another story, too. How I once had a hopelessly insecure friend who appeared to have everything: beautiful kids, a career, an inheritance. Yet, if something good came my way (my first book published, say), she would feign a smile, but I could see the scorn in her eyes. And it started to creep into the way I shared myself with her, and with others, too. I wondered, *is she the only one who feels this way?* I realized that whenever I was in her company, I made less of myself.

I am still not sure why that story popped into my head. But they really liked it.

And I liked telling it.

It made me see how fortunate I am today to know such self-assured people who have been at this much longer than I have, who get paid far more than I ever will. (I can still hope!) I am always amazed when, in the green room, they seem just as worried that they will, to quote one, "flounder like a fish and sink like a stone." I like being around people who know what it takes to prolong a creative life, who understand that having work we love *is* "all this." And more.

Then I backtracked a bit and shared how I once had so much to prove—to others, to myself—but not anymore. I emphasized that *this* is the kind of self-esteem I am after.

Nods in all directions. Jingle. Jingle. Jingle.

To wrap things up, I said, "This may sound cliché, but the moment is all any of us have. And there will always be the one who wants to snatch it away because, I suspect, they haven't had a moment of their own to celebrate in far too long."

There was a hush.

Now, a hush can go either way.

Then . . . clapping all around. *Jingles* all around.

And because I had found the perfect note to end on, so perfect it surprised even me, I clapped, too.

Determined

THIS IS HOW DECEMBER, 2016 finds me: determined not to let disappointment crush my spirit. I am not going to spend the whole month this way, not having shopped for a single present for the people I love, not having *thought* about a single present, wrapped them, made them beautiful.

There is a tight sadness that clutches my chest when the future feels too dated, too narrow, and lately it is *so* tight I can't even cry. And it is not only sadness, but weirder kinds of behavior crop up.

Take today. Normally, I defy all household chores until after my writing time. But this morning I folded the laundry before going anywhere near my office. And once everything was folded, I picked up the pile and threw it against the wall. I re-folded it, but I called it all kinds of terrible names first.

My neighbor down the hall said, "Since there's no way out of this, I'm giving everyone alcohol this year."

And last weekend I did something I have not done in years. I was just awful. A friend said something that made me speak in a way that held a great deal of passion, sure, but it mostly reflected my fear. I blamed his decision not to vote for all that scared me, a feeble attempt at releasing my disappointment and needing to fling it *some*where. I apologized, but I spent the next days feeling remorseful, embarrassed, unable to excuse my behavior.

My response to times of high anxiety has always been to get as far away as possible. Since November, I spend a lot of time imagining a simpler lifestyle in a simpler place, preferably with no cable news.

But the subtle joys of the season are beginning to push their way through. Even if I cannot imagine celebrating, they *can*.

I have my friend Lori to thank.

Lori is serious about the holidays. She will not just fling a strand of twinkly lights over a miniature potted pine from Safeway and call it a day. She is a decorating aficionado. As soon as I am inside her door, I always think two things at once: one person's (mine) whole decorating effort would be another's (Lori's) just getting started.

I am so happy Lori does all this, that she bothers. What amazing good luck it feels like to be able to sit around a table and tell all the funny stories we probably told last year, but who cares? To share a feast as satisfying, well, I hesitate to use the word *spiritual.*But good food *is* divine and will always transcend politics.

Hopefully, in a few weeks my disappointment will ease some. What will likely happen is, upon waking, I will feel a sense of appreciation for all the good in the world. *Fearful*, I will say, *is not how you want to live, capisce? And DO NOT look to any news feed for the hope you need.*

I will not stay detached, though, it would make me even more sad to just give up.

But for the month of December, I want to listen for words that come only in silence, ones that most of us (minus corrupt presidents, greedy cartels, most of Congress, and too many shady corporations) long for: *Peace. Truth. Decency.*

Here We Are

I am not unlike many professional artists. My work means piecing together a career from teaching, publishing, speaking fees, grants, honorariums, and applying to choreograph in faraway places, which satisfies my addiction to traveling *and* my love of dancing.

This month I am in Kerikeri, New Zealand, the first studio on a North Island tour.

It is not every day that I get to teach Polynesians, so, quickly as possible, I am going to write this column and press SEND. My lodging doesn't have internet—possibly what I like most about it—so I'm sitting outside a private residence, pilfering the wireless, because I know that when a great story falls into your lap, you should never wait.

And I cannot wait to write about Talia (tah LEE ah).

Talia walked into the studio slowly, but I did not get the feeling it was because she is bigger than most people, only that she comes from a humid island in the middle of the Pacific and slowly is just how people move due to the heat.

"I know nothing about your kind of dancing," she said, swaying her hips, "I worry I make a fool of myself." But, wow, it didn't take long to see how there is nothing slow about the way she *dances*. I have never known anyone quite as big (she had to come in the door sideways) who is as light on their feet.

"She's amazing," I whispered to the director.

"We've had a lot of hula dancers from Samoa join our classes and so . . ." he hesitated, "we've had our floor reinforced."

I liked Talia right away. When I think more about why, I consider all the people who are moving to Seattle lately whose main goal is to make money, or they have already made lots of it and arrive with airs to match. But Talia has the humble nature of someone who has had to work physically hard to earn her place in the world, and I can identify with that.

I'm fascinated by her jet black braid winding into a bun on top of her head; by her long skirts in all colors of the rainbow worn by people back home in a parade maybe, but not out and about, not in my part of the city anyway . . . maybe in Fremont; by the way she places her hand in front of her mouth to hide her laughter because she naturally wants to laugh off her mistakes more than the rest of us. What she does next is rub one hand over her stomach while the other rubs the small of her back, as if trying to rub out the blunder.

It's the funniest thing.

I looked at Talia, saw how deeply she loves to dance, and I was reminded how women like her help show me the way. Adults who have kept the love of dance in their lives, who do not let that pot belly, or those gray hairs stop them. Women who believe, as much as I do, that when we dance, we live.

If I hold them up to the light, I see they are my traveling stars, my roving guides, my mobile tribe.

Wherever I go, there we are.

No Other Way

It felt like the most heart-wrenching political circus ever.

It took me until now to realize it will need to be something else, as well.

Demi pointe: supporting your body on the balls of your feet. I have had to do a lot of them lately, not to improve my relevé, but to relieve the cramps in my calves that come on when tension builds.

Today, after holding my heels up as high as I could for as long as I could, this came to me: *I will need to work harder at embracing the personal as well as the political differences of others, i.e., my friends.*

The same thought comes flooding in at the Korean women's spa after my friend cries out, "Ladies, we need this to forget what just happened!" She means the impeachment hearings but every time we spring for a massage lately, we need to assuage our fears about something just as troubling.

I open my eyes to peek at the woman stripped down to her bra and panties, who works vigorously to scrub dead cells off my bare body. (I silently pledge to tip big.) Warm buckets of water are thrown over a myriad of female shapes, sizes, and colors. I cannot help but take in how different our bodies are.

And yet, how *alike*.

There is nothing quite as eye-opening as the naked truth.

This vision of all our bodies as one is just what I needed. I will rely on it to guide me through my mental list of relationships I-need-to-accept-as-they-*are,* now more than ever.

Fortunately, I have always had a fierce work ethic; a little voice inside of me that will not give up. And she has decided that *this* year is going to be a huge lesson in embracing diversity no matter what those mean little men in the White House try to roll back.

So.

From this day forward I will accept my friend's decision to take Prozac instead of leaving the job she hates. Am I insensitive? No. I have been bolstering my friend's confidence for as far back as I can remember. I have never told her, but she is the only whiner I could ever tolerate. But I am done trying to "help" her.

I accept that another friend, rather than leave her husband who has cheated, oh, I've lost count how many times, has joined his fundamentalist church. Last time I made us dinner, she scooped up a plate of food "in service" before she sat down. That is what she said, "in service." How afraid for her those two words made me feel. Let me make this clear: the food was for her husband who was not present. When she asked me to attend her baptism, I said, "No thank you, but next time he cheats, I'll be here for you."

Risky on my part, but I detected more than a little relief on hers. You can only imagine the big fat liar her husband is.

When my friend who smokes pot every day says, "I can stop anytime I want," I do not shake my head for the hundredth time. Though her lungs are deceiving her not: she huffs and puffs like a much older woman.

When another says she thinks Trump is a good man who has been given a bad rap, I avoid the conversation-that-could-end-our-friendship. It may be just the sort of conversation our country needs more of but, frankly, I have lost my stomach for it.

I say nothing to my neighbor who will not recycle because, as he put it, "It doesn't help a damn thing." It sounded like he said it just to goad me. But, still, *zip*.

And I promise myself to spend more time with people who make me laugh. Because I love feeling, well, not happy, that is too ambiguous, but eagerly hopeful.

Eager hopefulness restores me.

So when my beautiful and enthusiastic friend, Salina, hesitant to invite me to her wedding, prefaced by saying "I know you are insanely busy, but . . ." I responded, "no no, I'm *sanely* busy. I do what I love, I'm flexible, I'll be there!"

Because after all the antagonism the last years have caused, after I look around in dismay, after I gasp, after I cry, I know that the best recourse is to be there for each other, to accept each other, love each other best we can.

Because there is no other way.

Because if we don't, we will be lost and lonely and without calm. Like living in a huge house full of lush furniture, and yet we cannot find a comfortable place to sit down.

Different Time, Same Story

It is hard to explain to people today, when it seems like everyone wants to visit Italy, that our neighbors once targeted my family *because* we are Italian.

We had only lived in rural Connecticut a few weeks.

Once my father saved enough money to leave our city apartment behind, off we moved to the cul-de-sac where people had larger houses but, I soon came to realize, smaller tolerance for people unlike themselves. Just weeks after we had moved in, someone painted "WOPS GO HOME!" on the side of my father's station wagon.

I think the way in which I perceived myself changed the moment I saw those words.

My mother said it had to be one of the neighbor kids. I remember her saying something like, "kids do terrible things."

But I did not believe it was a kid, not on your life. I was only five, but I'd already begun to notice grownup things, like a certain man in the neighborhood who shook his head whenever our family drove by. I could detect his contempt for all of the European struggles he never had to face and for all the *Europeans* he suddenly had to. Without his consent.

My father has said that imagining the "American dream" was the only thing that got him through the Second World War. Except he did not carry the streets-paved-in-gold illusion. He defined the "dream" as living in a peaceful country. I'll never forget the look that came over him when he saw the slur splattered on his car, as if part of his dream had been snuffed out like one of his cigars, as if he'd finally witnessed something he'd been afraid of all along.

It was a different time, of course, when lots of us still believed that police always did the right thing, and so my father might have pretended to agree with my mother's plea to call them, but he never did. He just got out the hose and a scrub brush.

And now I wonder: do we all see what we want to see, or can handle seeing, and sweep the rest under, scrub it away, so we can tell ourselves everything is fine, because "fine" is what we so desperately want?

That night, I heard my father cry. I had never imagined it possible for him to cry. If *he* needed to cry, nothing felt safe and sound. I buried my head in the pillow.

My mother cried too but I was used to that.

I wet my bed that night and continued to for the next year. Night after night, anxiety seeped through my sheets.

There were other clues that my father was a little less secure in the budding suburbs than he let on. He likes to say that everybody in this country loves to eat, but nobody wants to grow food. He was proud of his vegetable garden. Yet, he planted it on the side of our house, not in the sunnier front. I think it was because all of the men around us wore suits to work. My father wore overalls. He still does.

Today, with all of the renewed rhetoric and lack of compassion for immigrants, well, I hope something else my mother said is true: *this too shall pass.*

I have my reasons for why I did not change my surname once I married. But the memory of my father scrubbing the side of his Ford is one of the strongest.

Years later—and why dreams come to us when they do, I have no idea—I woke with a start after seeing my father scrub at his car again. Only this time he was singing "Ain't No Sunshine" a popular song at the time that even today has a strong effect on me. I am sure the song pervaded my subconscious because I was heartbroken at the time. My first boyfriend, Steven, had just broken up with me, and this is what a preadolescent crush can feel like: I thought I would just die without him.

But I must have detected that what my father missed was the sunshine of southern Italy, both literally and in the familiar snug warmth of a true sense of place.

I laid back down, shut my eyes, and I began recreating my life experience, as all artists do, by choreographing the Bill Withers song that I still love to dance to.

The body longs to remember.

Then, Only Then

It is not often that I get to see my friend Lynn. "Off on another adventure," is her recurring autoresponder. She is independently wealthy, and she travels a lot.

I am not independently wealthy, and I work a lot.

Before I go on, can I tell you something that I am really tired of?

I am tired of people whipping out their phone to share photos in the middle of a conversation. I *ooh* and *ahh* over every image, obligingly, but I cannot stop the sense that all those pixels keep us from something essential: ourselves.

I think of a time when no one could scroll endlessly through the past—no matter where, no matter when—and I think: I miss those days.

Still, this is not an opinion I often share. It is sort of like my cousin Mario who did time, I don't bring him up to just anyone.

The last time Lynn and I met for lunch one thing was pretty clear: her latest adventure is Instagram. "Why are you taking pictures of your salad?" I asked.

"To share with my daughter," she said and smiled at me.

"Surely she's seen a salad before."

"Not with nasturtiums!" And, like that, she begins to scroll through a million salad photos.

Okay, that is a slight exaggeration, but there were a lot.

My favorite dance teacher once said that most people are followers, monkey see, monkey do. "But an artist's job is to question everything." Honestly, that was all, positively *all*, she had to say. I have questioned copy-cat behavior ever since. It used to drive my mother crazy. "Can't you just go along with it like everyone else?" she would say. Often. About so many things. Triggering me to say, "Let us go over the facts again, mom, shall we? No. I. Cannot."

I still believe the best reason to come together is to ignore the rest of the world, not to be interrupted by it, and I did wind up saying as much to Lynn. "I want to share stories about what we're doing and what we want to do next, not look at salads and listen to pings from your daughter, which pretty much takes care of this time being *ours*. One ping is fine. But after that, it's too much."

And Lynn says, "Well. Fine. But I think you are overreacting."

I cringe at how wrong this conversation feels suddenly. But I have too many imaginings lately where everyone is recording everything, and no one is really *seeing*. "This worries me," I said to my husband.

"There'd be something wrong with you if you weren't worried," he said.

I think what is happening is that I have learned to recognize when something has gone too far, when, no matter how much money it makes for some, it's just not better for everyone, especially anyone with addictive tendencies. You figure this out pretty quickly when your friend who has fought long and hard to give up alcohol is snapping photo after photo of arugula greens.

Finally, she put her phone on the table face up. I reached over and put it face down.

"You seem different," she said. "As much of a pain as ever, but more of a stickler."

My mind flicked through what she just said for something to refute it. (I wish I could say this is not stickler behavior, but it is.) "Well," you may be right," I said, "but are so many photos really necessary? Do they make you happier than just sitting back and enjoying yourself?"

"Well, they don't make me any less happy."

It was such an honest thing to say, any objection stuck in my throat. I couldn't help but soften. Personal honesty exceeds all. Exceeds everything we would eventually talk about and any photo taking, certainly.

"Well—" I let the word hang in the air for a moment, "now that your phone isn't having more fun than we are, I get to hear you say the kind of brilliant things I love you for."

"You're right about that at least. I am brilliant."

Then, only then, we begin to catch up with *us*, finally sharing the kind of connection that all those photos are *supposed* to bring to the table.

But, sadly, do not.

And if I find myself left out of all the photos she loves to post, I have only myself to blame.

Pummi's Salmon Recipe

All morning, I have been trying to write about the delicate issue of diet, but it hasn't been fun, and here's why: people ask me all the time, "what do you eat?" And then they don't want to know.

My friend Pummi asked me just the other day, in fact, right after she threw a copy of *Vogue* on the table with a smack.

I leaned over and pushed the magazine to the floor.

And though my closet is testament to a life-long devotion to certain classic fashions, I do not read fashion magazines. I no longer enjoy images of clothes that belong only to the youngest of us. It feels like too much effort to work through the loss I feel.

I would rather outsource working through the loss I feel. If only I could.

What I did not know was that giving up the magazines would be harder than I thought, like quitting a sugar addiction. I miss certain things about escaping the world with glossy fantasy, so I did have a brief flirtation with *More* before it went under. I liked that it claimed to be for "women of substance."

Assuming, of course, they meant me.

But when I leafed through, I was reminded of all the many ways women shell out big bucks for younger skin, and I do not believe we can have younger skin. I think the best we can do is look like we are trying for younger skin, sometimes too hard.

Besides, a few wrinkles around the eyes shows that we are women who have laughed and lived, and I don't even know *what* to think about bleaching our teeth so white they glow like moons in the dark.

The only article I found with any real substance was one disastrous account of learning the hard way that just because a "treatment" can be done does not mean it is botch proof. I had not given any thought to "resurfacing" my face before. I thought resurfacing was for asphalt.

It was a desperate story of personal tragedy.

I rather enjoyed it.

As I write this, the sun is brilliant outside. The first time I met Pummi was on a day like this. When she first emigrated to Seattle from Mumbai, she was trim and fit. Walking toward me on 4th Avenue in a festive yellow sari, even the sidewalk seemed to brighten with her presence. I remember thinking how she struck me so differently than, say, the somberness I feel when I pass a woman wearing a black niqab. Though, to be clear, I don't feel somber about the woman *underneath* the cloth. That one of these women, new to my block, has eyes that open wide whenever we meet, always makes me think, *I would like to see more of you.* And when we do share a few words, she listens in a focused way I find harder and harder to come by.

It is a rare quality, listening and then talking, instead of the other way around.

These days Pummi wears jeans like pretty much everyone else. And she is no longer trim and fit. She is *ample.* Or the word we use when we will not willingly say "fat," not caring what anyone thinks.

I write from memory, so when Pummi asked me about my diet, comparing my body to a mixing spoon, "you are like this," she said, holding up a spoon, "skinny all the way up to your head," I remember thinking something like, *well, I've never been compared to a utensil before.*

She used to cook me these amazing, curried vegetable dishes. But after a year of living in this country, she must have decided that cows were no longer sacred because suddenly it was all beef this and beef that. And "American potatoes." Not baked potatoes, or mashed, but fries. Homemade fries with saffron, but still.

Which leads me to Pummi's salmon recipe.

Now, writing about Pummi's salmon recipe *is* fun.

"Well," I said, tentatively, "I tend to eat more vegetables and fish."

"Oh, I eat fish!" she said in that excited way she speaks whenever she speaks about food. "I will cook you my new salmon recipe, yes?"

Honestly, it was *the* most tender-crispy salmon I have ever tasted. "Just sprinkle with herbs and broil," she said.

So that's what I did. Except my salmon was not tender. My salmon was not crispy brown. We were okay, my dry-slab-of-salmon and me, but I missed my way of steaming it into lemony-moist perfection.

"Really?" I pressed. "Just herbs?" I desperately wanted to say what I suspected.

"Well, yes," she said.

"Nothing else?"

Now, you have to imagine her saying what she said next in her most melodious Mumbaikar accent, "Just herbs . . ." Pause. "And a stick of melted butter, yes?" She took a step back.

I became a low-fat eater years ago, and, like many converts, an ardent one. So, it did occur to me to say that we do not need butter to cook salmon, it has plenty of its own flavor and fat.

Instead, I changed the subject.

And as a result, I did not make one of the biggest mistakes that is possible between friends.

Now and again, I still like to write about healthy eating habits for certain publications, sharing what has worked for me with interested readers. But not with my friends.

I raise my voice in defiance to anyone who thinks it is okay to tell someone we love what to eat. It is not "for their own good. We are not "only trying to help." It is a vain act. And I am finding it harder and harder to forgive myself for anything that smacks of "vain" lately.

But this is not why I gave up the fashion magazines. I gave them up because I miss being young enough to feel *entitled* to vanity.

Oh! There are times when the truth unfolds so visibly, like a bud into bloom.

Like walking into a garden full of rich colors and silky textures, and it's all so beautiful you can't find the precise word for the way it stings.

Before you feel suddenly at peace.

There Goes the Neighborhood

I WAS REMEMBERING SOMETHING I heard the other day on the sidewalk: "I'm a writer," the woman said into her phone, "I don't see the point in *not* writing. Screw emoji."

All my life, I have loved hearing people talk this openly.

It happened again at a little wine shop in the Market where I realized that if I kept my head down, I might get to hear the entire exchange: "No, I am *not* doing eyelash extensions!" one woman said to another.

I was all ears.

"Because if *that* is what women are doing these days, they can fight that fight anyway they like. I have a lot of insecurities, but not about my eyelashes."

It was not an earth-shattering admission. Not like when I had to admit in front of a well-informed audience (after declaring, "Oh! No! We cannot leave NATO!") that I had absolutely no idea what NATO stands for, who belongs to it, or what they do, exactly.

But when someone has the guts to push back against the latest trend—I have noticed excessively-long eyelashes are everywhere lately—that makes us feel as though we are never good enough as we are, I feel nothing but gratitude.

My friends and I talk a lot about this, how sometimes we just need to push back against popular trends, beauty and otherwise. I mean, our first life lesson is resistance. As soon as we learn to say "no" we learn how to speak up and not cower.

So, this morning, at two a.m., the sleeping woman I usually am at this hour decided—after a talk with myself that went something like *if you don't say something, you won't be able to forgive yourself, but if you do, get ready, because you'll probably suffer the outcome just as much*—to pound on my neighbor's door to object to the loud music.

Wait, did I just say "neighbor?" Because I do not have a neighbor.

I used to have a neighbor. His name was Dean. We shared a wall for six years. We looked out for each other. I was surprised, outraged, when his landlord served him notice in order to turn his apartment into a vacation-rental.

Apartment by apartment, my Belltown building has become less of a vertical neighborhood and more of a hotel. Problem is, people tend to party late in hotels, even on weeknights, while residents need to go to work in the morning.

I was working in San Francisco when vacation rentals were a city-wide debate. In the Mission, I listened to a group of Latinos talk about losing their hotel jobs. Not to work in hotels is an incomprehensible way to live for these people. VRBO and Airbnb are affecting their livelihood in ways I had not thought about before. Heading out the door, I heard a man say, "no one is going to tell me I can't rent out my place in the city while I'm at my lake house in Tahoe."

There were at least three other things this man said that made me see how his argument summed up so many of the inequities of contemporary life. How those with less charmed lives, without a spare house, or even a spare room, still need to work physically hard in exchange for a paycheck.

Still, I doubt the man who is buying up condos in our building in order to turn them into short-term rentals would consider himself someone contributing to the lack of affordable housing, but, in a less talked-about way, he is.

The trend is everywhere. It is not limited to cities.

And it's funny because in Airbnb promotions they like to boast how you get to "live in a real neighborhood." And it's the *way* they say it. As if you can just plop yourself down as soon as you figure out the key code and *belong*.

When my friend and her infant son needed to find an apartment in a small town on the Olympic Peninsula, there were only four long-term rentals available. Yet, on the same town's vacation-rental websites, there are literally hundreds of listings.

And try as I might, I cannot see a real neighborhood in that.

∾

I realize I have taken on two separate issues here and failed to fuse them together neatly, all essay-like.

Fortunately, certain failures lose their bite over time.

There are days I just want to throw on the color like an abstract painter and see what happens. Days when my writing time can fly by so fast and I cannot seem to hang on to any one concern.

And I don't *want* to.

Not that I mean to raise a third issue.

Ridiculous

Say what you will about people's reactions to refugees around the world, but you cannot say they are lacking in insensitivity.

I cannot believe some of the heartless, unsympathetic things I hear people say lately.

It is so awful to ridicule people who are just trying to stay alive. It is the worst unfairness, like kicking a lost puppy.

I think most of the problem is sheer forgetfulness. History has taught us that prejudice is like the wind. One day it is directed away from us. The next, it comes at us out of nowhere. With a vengeance.

But we tend to forget that part.

This is my friend's own truth. Coming of age in Italy at a time when most of Europe turned its back on Jewish people, "even me," he admits, "I was ignorant," he soon landed in the bowels lower Manhattan where, if Italians dared to venture north of Houston, people really did throw rotten tomatoes. In no time, he changed his name from Tommaso to Tom, his hat from flat cap to fedora.

It's funny what a history buff you become after learning about your people's ingenuity. Ask me anything, anything at all, about past prejudices in the world.

My point is—walls do not work. Whether they are made of steel or fruit, people find another way.

My own coming of age? On my first day of college, my father forbade me letting any boy into my dorm room. *Ever.*

I think the less specifically said about this the better.

But the reason I am remembering it and trying to jot it down quickly so that I can enjoy the rest of my day at the beach, is that to my left sits a woman wearing a hijab. And because it is one of our rare 80-degree days, I think, *oh, honey, it is so hot today. And your husband wears H&M shorty-shorts. How is that fair?*

I even answer my own question. *It is not fair.*

I want to wave a magic wand that allows her to feel the breeze on her skin.

What I really want is for her to yank off the smoldering cloth and run splashing into Puget Sound so I can cheer the way other people cheer on the Mariners.

Still, I would never want to ban the hijab, even from schools. Though, to be honest, I don't mind a public outcry now and again when we sense another way of teaching women to feel less powerful.

I've written before about the chador and the hijab, and all this time since, I have never been able to fully understand what determines a woman's right to choose her own clothing vs. what appears like out and out control of her choices, even if she willingly abides. I am not proud of the way I still want to look down when these black- swathed women pass me on the sidewalk so that I'm not tempted to say, "Do not accept this, it's demoralizing."

To this day, I ask myself *if looking down disrespects them. Or you?*

Both, I think.

I decide to wander a little. Clear my head.

When I get to the woman's blanket, I am not sure why it feels impossible to reign in my inclination to probe, "It's such a warm day, isn't it?"

"No," she replied.

No?

At once, I had two thoughts. One was that she sounded like she had been waiting for someone to walk up and disapprove. How awful it must be to feel like others are judging you, feeling sorry for you.

The other was that I realized what a mistake I had made. If there had been an escape hatch beneath me, I would have pulled the cord and quickly tunneled back to Belltown.

Did I really think I could walk right up and give rise to some new form of equality she has not considered? And that she would want to veto everything she has been taught since birth and shift directly from her viewpoint to mine?

Doesn't this sound so insular and narrow and flat out ridiculous of me?

Of course it does.

As insular and narrow and flat out ridiculous as a border wall.

Why Is It?

LAST NIGHT I WAS CHATTING to a neighbor about this and that when he said, "It's all a big conspiracy anyway."

Now, I like delving into the mind of another as much as the next person, maybe even more, so I might have asked, "What is?"

Except the last time I gave a conspiracy theorist an opening like this, I was sharing a seat on the #2 bus with a woman who looked upset that I didn't know the government is spreading mind-altering chemicals out of airplanes. I thought about interrupting her to say, "Do you mean contrails? Contrails are condensation." Except conspiracy theorists tend to want to control the conversation, not listen, I have noticed that.

I headed for another seat.

"And . . ." she yelled back, squinting an eye at me, "they are taking cursive away so when the power goes out, we won't be able to communicate!"

Suddenly the bus did not feel big enough for all the doom she wanted to spread. I was nearly at the end of my rope when my new seat mate leaned over and whispered, "Just ignore her. That's what we do."

I tried to ignore her, but a few things caught my eye.

One was that her shoes were Stuart Weitzman, her handbag was Louis Vuitton, and her sunglasses? Tom Ford, $495.00 retail. Another was that she got off the bus in *upper* Queen Anne, an expensive, sociable neighborhood that always makes me feel like living in an affordable high-rise in impersonal Belltown is not really living at all. I was left wondering why conspiracy theorists are generally the most well-off people I meet.

One of the most wonderful parts of my work as a dance teacher is that it has brought me to the far corners of the world. The woman on the #2 bus made me remember an expat couple who lived in a beautiful home on the beach on the island of St. Croix, nothing to want for, nothing to fear.

Except they did.

They feared everything—the local people, local authorities, local dogs, dog bites, dog *poo*.

And viruses. Especially "government cooked-up viruses."

At first, they seemed sort of well-informed, but as the conversation wore on, I realized they were getting crazier by the minute. They started to sound less like residents with useful information to share, and more like a couple of drunks convinced that the end of the world is near. With each whiff of alcohol on their breaths, there were even stronger traces of apocalypse. And that is not what I wanted my time on the island to be about.

I know theories do not hurt people; people hurt people. But so does fear.

I once met a woman in Sequim so far into apocalypse-theory, her fourteen-year-old daughter committed suicide to avoid it.

So, I am curious. Was all their fear a metaphor for being unable to make peace with their good fortune? For unfulfilled dreams or mistakes made? Or for never having found work they enjoy, or creative expression? Is this what happens when too much time is spent looking backward from a bar stool? Are conspiracy theorists disillusioned, bored, isolated, lonely, passing too many hours on the internet? All of the above?

On the other hand, the local people of St. Croix— much like people I've met in other places in the world where no one can afford much—are quick to share one pair of dilapidated ballet slippers between multiple dancers, and even quicker to say things like, "Thank you! Sweet Lord! Thank you! We are blessed to have these dance shoes! Uh, huh. Blessed!"

When the boozy couple could not agree if the next "real" war will be with the Muslims or with China, my response was to remind them that some 35,000 people die annually on average from gun-related injuries in the U.S. "And if that isn't a *real* war, I don't know what is," I said, knowing it was pointless to argue.

It felt good, though.

But only until I remembered there are so many wars raged on so many fronts already, so why start another?

Quickly, calmly, I excused myself.

ON A CLEAR SEPTEMBER NIGHT

THE MOON ROSE OVER a crystal blue lake.

No sky could be more expressing of why, the first time I saw Lake Crescent, I stayed for three months, living about as far west as one can travel in this country without quite leaving it. I swam in the lake, bathed in it, fell in love with my husband in a tiny cabin on its south shore.

And I came to know, or thought I did, why the first recorded interpretation of the Holy Spirit was not man-like in nature, but "spiritual" as the word applies to water, "giver of all life." I remember reading this and feeling I had finally found a faith that made sense to me: *We begin in water. Water is holy.*

Yes, yes, I thought, *I am a believer.*

But the lake is not my story here. Anna is my story.

Also, Womenfest.

Womenfest is an annual celebration on Lake Crescent's northeast shore, where women from all over the state of Washington gather in an outdoor retreat center named Camp David . . . though I seriously wish they would *re*name it.

And what is so completely true about this gathering is that the women who attend have been through careers and kids and marriages and divorces. In other words, we have all had to learn—and *re*learn—how less easy we make things for ourselves when we do not trust ourselves more.

I was invited to give a reading. I felt myself surrender to the sheer good feeling of sharing my work.

But something bad happened.

Before it did, I said that a writer does not write to convince anyone of anything, but to figure out how *we* feel. Then I shared an Op-Ed I wrote back in April 2003 (how long we've been at war in the Middle East!) that ended: "If a woman suffers because her brother, husband, or son might come home prone in a vinyl bag, I support her and politics be damned. That's enough certainty to keep me sane through all this."

The room went still, a good still, full of acquiescence.

And then, like an arrow, someone shot from the room.

Even if I have gotten better over the years at not taking quick exits personally, I would be lying if I said the speed of the woman's exit didn't bother me. Not only did everyone look in her direction, but this kind of interruption means I will have to work doubly hard to win the audience back. It can make even the most seasoned speaker lose focus. And if your focus fails, it shows.

Later, I learned the woman's name was Anna and that she lives in Port Angeles where a lot of boys grow up to view the military as a career path. She and I sat on either side of a picnic table. "I'm sorry," she said, "but

I lost a nephew in Iraq. My son came home disabled. I hardly know him now he is so medicated."

Her words echoed way beyond what she said.

I closed my eyes. And what came into focus was this: Because we have stopped assuming the truth is being told about these useless wars, we rarely get it. Anna made me face these wars again, made me realize that I have grown too used to war like everyone else. Numb.

Now, I am angry again.

And this is good! Anger is so often criticized, but there are times we need more of it.

Eventually, Anna and I laughed about something or other, and then we hugged each other goodbye.

The drive out of town was eerie. I had this devastating sense of being a mother in Port Angeles while the child I have raised goes out into the world and never comes back.

I did not think I believed in such things, but a wisp of smoke rose over town and hovered. It was only mill smoke, but within its swirls I saw a stream of enlisted kids, I swear I did, rolling down the sidewalk on skateboards, pumping up the hills on bikes.

And just before the exit to Highway 101, I heard the voice of a young man say, *Hey, check it out! There's Civic Field where we used to play baseball, remember? And the elementary school hasn't changed a bit. And there's my skateboard overturned on the lawn. I guess I forgot to put it away.*

Sorry, mom.

Having Said That . . .

I ENJOY SHARING THE UPS and downs of a writing life no matter who extends the invitation.

And I do not mean to exclude any one group from the above statement, but the academic world, I must tell you, is not my favorite audience.

When I arrive, there are generally smiles of greeting, handshakes, even hugs. But academia has a way of making me feel sized up before I even take off my coat.

A wise friend put it like this: "Academia is all about climbing the next rung, elbowing your way through, getting tenured. And you are free of all that. You are out there, enthusiastic and determined, and that's deeply rankling to some."

Occasionally, you get the perfect pep talk.

She did not stop there. "There will always be some who'd rather tear you down, there is solidarity in that. Like agents, academics are eager to be seen as independent, but they conform to a strict line. And they can begrudge individualists they'd rather *be*."

This made me remember a woman at my last talk who stood up and introduced herself at length, telling everyone she was a professor of English and that she edits a literary journal. Let me make this clear: this would be like introducing yourself to a Barista by explaining that you know a thing or two about making coffee, too.

"And what you said about confidence is interesting," she said, settling her gaze on the audience without even looking at me. "Having said that . . . "

It was after her second "having said that" that I began to twitch.

After her third, she brought back an affection for my father's way of dealing with "know-it-alls" (basically, anyone with a better vocabulary than his). He'd throw up his hands and yell "shaddap!" indicating he was in no mood.

I bit my tongue and thought, *okay, let's wrap this up, shall we? I could use a drink. Who's in?*

When I think back to the next even more irritating thing she said about some other writer's approach to confidence, and how mine "seemed contradictory in comparison," I wish I had said, "Oh no you don't! I do not do that. I do not compare my writing to anyone else's so why should you? It's just another way of trying to impress your peers, but it has nothing to do with me. Writing is what I love to do, so I do it. And when I am asked to share it, it is icing on the cake. And you are ruining my cake!"

I keep going over in my head what else I would have said if I hadn't run out of time (and nerve) to tell my truth as it is: "Most days I start off confident, but after I've put in the hours, I can start to feel like I'm losing it. And this always reminds me how fit my mental health has to be to repeatedly drive myself crazy like this. So, yes, I *am* a contradiction." Pause. "And if you don't yet understand this inner conflict, I promise, you will."

I arrived at my speaking career through the back door, and before anyone could decide what it is that I was doing, I was already doing it. Plus, I like to make my audience laugh so when one member of the local literati labeled me "a performer, basically," I thought, *I'm fine with that*. I don't think he would sink so low as to compare me to, say, a standup comedian, but *having said that*, I am not embarrassed to be "highly accessible" either.

Motivational speakers don't take me all that seriously, either. I am fluff to them.

When the professor was finally finished addressing the room, I could see that proving me "less than" gave her "more of" whatever she so desperately needed. Without missing a beat, I told everyone to give her a hand. I wanted to be unpretentious, generous; anything that made me different from her.

I have a friendly neighbor, Marie, who, after I told her about the evening, dubbed the woman as "a good old-fashioned teacher."

"How so?" I asked, knowing Marie used to teach high school.

"A relentless need to instruct. We *ache* to instruct."

This made me think of my mother-in-law, also a retired teacher, and how she used to mail my letters back, red-lined with grammatical corrections.

She went on to say that the professor probably began her life as an inquisitive child, but how so many things can chip away at a woman's confidence until, in spite of herself, she has become an insecure adult.

She says things like this, and I listen.

When Marie shares her opinion, she instructs, yes, but with foresight. And though there have been a few times when I don't exactly appreciate the foresight, it continually points the way toward a new perspective. Even flustered, I can see that.

I think this has always been my basic wish for conversation, that I find one thing in any of it that helps me see beyond. And when I do find one thing, I do not respond to it on a purely rational level.

It's a deeper effect.

Like how I was taught as a child to sense the communion wafer.

Let it lie on your tongue for as long as possible before you swallow any of it.

And So, I Write

Fourteen years ago, while Seattle was still reeling from The Jewish Federation shooting, I intentionally wrote a light-hearted column for December. It seemed like a good idea at the time. I figured we all needed a break.

Eight years ago, while the world was still reeling from Sandy Hook, I wrote another "uplifting" column.

I was so far down, each word strove to bring me up.

Both columns remind just how far I was willing to go to leave reality behind.

Winston Churchill said that if you are going through hell, keep going. I feel this way about writing. With each new shooting, I feel too shattered to write, yet it is my only relief. Deep breaths do not make me feel any better. Digging my nails into the sides of my cheeks doesn't help either. Stretching helps. A little. It doesn't last, but it's crucial that I find a barre to hold on to. And fast.

Because you cannot laugh when you are lifeless inside, but you can write.

You can sit down to what you know is going to be a rough ride, your mind drifting all over the place while you try not to let your thoughts fall into the gravest space of your deepest fears.

There are so many similarities between the gun-disheartenment I feel today, and the head-banging defeat I felt at the scene of The Jewish Federation: I hope this shooting is the last shooting and, at the same time, I know that it won't be until the veins in my neck start to bulge.

Then, when the next shooting *does* happen, I feel as though I know all I need to know without needing to tune in or read about it. The worst part of it is, I am not as shaken to the core.

And so, once again, I will share one of my lighter tributes to the season of hope, partly out of news-cycle-fatigue, and partly out of a desire to think about something as emotionally simple as gift giving. Because today it feels like the thoughtful, caring, daughter I am inside needs to live only for her mother's favorite holiday.

Then again, so do I.

Here is my regift, then, told with the same amount of pleasure.

At the Big Picture on 1st Avenue, I sit next to a woman I have seen around Belltown for years, a woman I take note of because she reminds me of my mother. While waiting for the film to begin, I go over and over in my head why this is, since she does not look anything *like* my mother.

Manner. That's what it is. The word that always makes me think of what my Aunt Connie used to say while applying her lipstick: *per fare bella figura*—to make a good showing. She never left the house without rosy lips.

Let's just say that if this woman and my mother were to chat about family, religion, or politics—though they would likely skip religion and politics—they would agree about most things, or politely pretend to. They are mothers from the same era. And even if they have no more in common than having babies in the fifties, this becomes its own loyalty in the same way veterans bond over a shared war.

And if December was *not* about finding the perfect gift for those we love, I would be satisfied with a quick scan of this woman before leaning back to enjoy the trailers.

But I believe in inklings. I am always on the lookout for them. So, I study her a while longer. This time, like a portrait.

And once I see beyond the form and color, there it is.

Oh, no! What was I thinking?

See, just yesterday I bought my mother a lovely silk blouse at Nordstrom. But the blouse is an utterly inappropriate gift for my mother. The blouse is appropriate for, you guessed it, *me*. What my mother would love is a red sweatshirt with the words "World's Greatest Grandmother" stitched to its bodice. She delights in bragging about her grandchildren.

Let us back up a little.

I need to back up here and admit something I am not especially proud of. I have been trying (and failing) to remake my mother for most of my life. And after I learned to understand and even forgive this about myself, I got on with accepting my mother for who she really is. I just had to drop all the silly, overly sensitive expectations and think *woman to woman*.

And so, if at first I didn't understand why this woman was affecting me, I do now: to remind me to return the blouse. Tomorrow. First thing.

Because there is a real message here even for the most irreverent: Gift giving is about the person on the *receiving* end.

As soon as the movie is over, I'll surf the net until I find the sweatshirt. Because of all the people I need to buy for, mom is the one I most want to please.

Mom is always the one I most want to please.

Which this year I fully intend to do.

~

It's been a wretched year.

And yet, and *yet*, there are so many stories that uplift.

And so, I write.

A Sturdier Place

My friend Steve and I are on our first loop around Green Lake, our favorite meeting place to walk and talk, sometimes without even needing to say much.

It is one of those unexpectedly warm winter afternoons that makes everyone feel lighter. The clouds cut across the sky so that the lake glows one moment and looks shaded the next. I feel as relaxed as I have in a long time.

Funny how this is. You begin your walk feeling doubtful, but after circling the lake's path, you have restored faith in the path *you* are setting.

By our second loop, it is nearly sunset. "The hour of truth," Steve calls it and I can tell when his truth is not so much about to surface but burst. I love when this happens. It generally means I am about to get a history lesson. Political history is Steve's thing. I can practically see his wheels turning backward in time and how happy remembering our forefathers makes him.

We did not come to Green Lake the day after Pete Buttigieg dropped out of the race. We walked along the waterfront, but only to the sculpture park. "I should write a song about this day," Steve said. "A sad song about shortsightedness."

Today—I think because we live in fear of November 3rd but do not want to talk about it—our lesson is about Thanksgiving. It was, he says, an English harvest celebration held the first week in October as it still is in Canada. And the reason why ours is now on the third Thursday in November is that in 1941, the U. S. Congress passed an act declaring it so. Federal workers pointed out that October has Halloween; December has Christmas; January has New Year's. Obviously, something had to be done about November, and the third Thursday has a good ring to it. Congress agreed.

"Well, why wouldn't they?" I say.

Next, we get to talking about a mutual friend we lost to cancer. Which leads to a discussion about other friendships. Ones we love who love us back.

And ones who break our hearts.

I held my breath and thought about one friend who decided not to be my friend anymore, withdrawing with no explanation. It left me trying to figure out what terrible thing I had done. "I cringe now at how confused I was. For months I was afraid to reach out to anyone new," I said.

"Well, it's always good to reflect before charging ahead," Steve says, thinking more, I'm sure, about the marriage he had to let go of and can still get angry about even after twenty years.

But that's the way he is. More often than not, Steve speaks objectively.

Not surprisingly, my friend Diane rushes into mind. "She certainly taught me that it's possible to keep someone close after letting them go," I say, after sharing what happened. Again. My side of the story. Vividly.

But as Dionne Warwick says, that's what friends are for.

Steve calls my attachment to Diane an emotional deep state. "When habits rule," he says, putting his arm around me briefly.

"You would describe love like that, wouldn't you?" I say, and to change the subject, I remind him that since our last visit, I had addressed my first international conference and he hadn't asked me about it yet. "Some friend," I say.

"You're brave," is all he says.

"Brave, me? No way. If you knew what I looked like in the greenroom, I doubt you would think I was brave. I was terrified. I picked every piece of fuzz off the couch and then I started on the floor."

He crinkles his eyes fondly.

"And it's weird because I've chosen performance anxiety pretty much my whole life. When I was a kid, I'd stage puppet shows for the relatives. Italian relatives. Very judgmental."

"You just knew you wanted to run your own show," he says. "And earn your own pennies."

"Yep. Pennies for pay. That's the part that has stayed the same."

We talk about when we had last seen so-and-so and what they are up to. We talk about virus-related things, too, mostly old-fashioned remedies. This exchange went something like: "It's like we won't be allowed to cough anymore, run a fever, and heaven help us if we sneeze in public," Steve says, and I say my Chinese friend believes in herbs that smell terrible, and he says his "Amazonian" neighbor makes green pot squares made with avocado instead of butter, and I say my Austrian friend said a shot of schnapps "chases off the bug" and that I have no problem with her advice whatsoever, and he says his sister calls chicken soup nature's antibiotic.

And that brought me to my Filipino neighbor Marlin ("like the fish," she said when we met) who swears by slow cooked beef tongue.

"Ew," I said.

"No, ew!" she yelled. "Just do it!"

I love Marlin. What I know about the kind of friendship we share—how affection can express itself as a command, how it isn't all that easy to "just do it" but do it we must—I learned from her.

"Now *that* kind of attachment is healthy," Steve says. "And a fine example of," he thinks for a moment, "bipartisanship."

"Minus the politics," I said.

"Nothing is minus the politics," he said.

I spent the next couple of minutes thinking *this* is how his mind works to make the world a sturdier place: it's all about the roots.

The roots of language.

The roots of behavior.

The roots of past decisions and how they lead to future progress.

Hopefully.

And I always have to ask myself, after a walk with Steve, how any denial of roots whatsoever could be any way to grow.

A Lifelong Lesson (Forever. Continuously.)

How can I begin to answer my eighty-year-old friend's question about what it means to be "true to my country?"

"Barbara," I say, "all I know is that if I listen to our president speak, I get such an empty feeling. Now, saying *that* feels true, if not to my country, at least to myself."

It's easy to see disapproval in Barbara's eyes.

Honestly, the world Barbara lives in is not a place I know very well. When she invited me to speak to her book club nine years ago, I remember the first stupid thing I said was, "Wow! My entire place would fit into your foyer."

Even so, every so often she still invites me to lunch.

And we still enjoy our conversations—the openness, the frank confrontations—because that is ultimately what we wind up sharing, a good sparring that includes huge differences of opinions that make us think the other is crazy. Even more that make us fonder of each other. Our cross-generational friendship may hold within it some of the most challenging conversations I've ever had.

Still, I am a little intimidated by Barbara.

In fact, every part of me flinches because I know her allegiance to our asinine president is set in stone and there's no easy way to convey what *my* allegiances are, if I have any, which, to Barbara, apparently I do not.

"Barbara? You say you love this country, but it sounds like you flat out dislike most of the newcomers in it. Especially those who do the hard-physical work you would never dream of doing, like massaging your body at that spa you love so much or mowing your lawn. Is that what I'm hearing?"

It was a tough question. But no tougher than hers to me.

And here is what she said, and how we each tried to hold our tongues afterwards, "You always over-simplify the issues."

Always? The next few moments passed nerve-rackingly slow.

But I knew not to push. I know how it can be between friends, one too many push backs is like one too many dropped stitches. Before the whole weave unravels.

And yet, I expect this level of honesty from Barbara. I would go so far as to say I visit *because* of it. The more I stood there thinking about the fact that we can say things like this to each other and remain friends, well, my thoughts turn from, oh, I don't know, *cold hard carbon into a diamond*? Big as the diamond Barbara wears.

Yes, this comparison will do.

Really, Barbara's wedding ring is the classic epitome of riches, assets, *means*.

"Politics divides people, Barbara. So, I'm going to kiss your forehead and leave now."

"Since we're apologizing, I'll just say boy was I right about you."

I braced myself. *Oh, god, here it comes. But don't worry, friendship is like the tide. It comes in. It goes out. You'll be fine. You'll get over it.*

"You *are* wise beyond your years." She walked over and gave me a hug. A real hug. Not a usual-Barbara hug. Which is more of a pat on the back.

With our weave stronger, our diamonds gleaming, I rinsed off my plate and headed out the door, noting to myself how everything at that moment felt balanced as the palm trees that grow in two huge pots to frame Barbara's front door. They look so out of place in Seattle, but this is one opinion I will never share with her. I made myself *promise*.

I think of those green plumes now, tall, tough, commanding.

Waving hello.

Waving goodbye.

Or, as Barbara would say, ta-ta.

∾

A few weeks after this conversation with Barbara, I was a guest teacher in Melbourne, Australia where the subject of immigration is also in hot debate. One woman I talked to was from Italy. "This is a good country," she said, "but it has too many immigrants."

"But *you* are an immigrant," I said.

She just stared at me. And I'd bet my life she was thinking: *But I'm white.*

I left her thinking *it's the same hypocrisy everywhere.*

Later in a café, I met a woman from Iran. "I'll do anything to hold on to my freedom," she said. "Anything."

Now, you may want to cover your ears when I tell you what she does for a living. "I sell my used underwear on-line," she said. It wasn't even a big deal for her to tell me. "When I go to the gym, I wear two pairs under my tights."

I tried hard not to make a face. I tried even harder to stop thinking about the kind of man who buys her panties. Mostly, I realized that within minutes of meeting someone, everything about your idea of independence can change.

I will not share this story with Barbara. I know the truest thing about our bond, any bond, is that it is both strong and delicate—a tension for two.

I always think about this kind of equilibrium when I think of Barbara.

I think: *This is where I pull. This is where I release.*

REACH OUT

I HAVE BEEN LYING ON THE COUCH, sick with the flu, the coughing, lightheaded, feverish flu that you have either caught by now or fear that you will. I have not been outside in days. I can barely sit up long enough to write this.

I know to rest, drink plenty of liquids, be *patient*.

But I will never be a patient sick person. I want to be a patient sick person, patient enough to luxuriously catch up with Netflix, patient enough to make homemade soup. Patient enough to put my work aside and surrender without fear or complaint.

But none of this is easy for me. I get so bored watching TV and I have a short attention span in the kitchen. Sick as I am, I take my seat at my desk and try to think of something worth thinking about.

I even marvel at my effort.

But let's be serious, I can't even remember what day of the week it is. I am just going to have to trust that my mental ability will come back.

Who knows when, but it will.

In the meantime, I have an elderly neighbor who is sicker than I am. I know because I can hear him coughing through the wall we share. It is the same cough I have, but raspier. It reminds me of something my mother said years ago. She was coughing and coughing and crying out to my dad that she was too young to die.

And he said, "You are already too old for that."

Strangely, she did not react. I think she had spent so many years being annoyed at him for one thing or another and she just didn't have the energy to be annoyed anymore. I felt so bad for her, I sat on the bed and rubbed her back.

Now, here is something I *can* do. I can bring my neighbor a bowl of the not-too-terrible soup I made (almost) from scratch. Because this flu, it is not just the flu, people, it is so much worse. And while most of my neighbors are not elderly and living alone, this man is, and it's only been a month since his partner of thirty years died.

They used to hold hands in the elevator and just being in their presence made you feel a validation of never-giving-up on someone you love. Even if you have been burned one too many times, one look in their direction and it's like your stubborn little heart rips right open. Another neighbor took one look at them in the elevator and blurted out, "God, I am so jealous."

When I knocked on my neighbor's door and said, "Seems we're in this flu thing together," you should have seen the look on his face. It was next to nothing on my part, really. Even with my head about to explode, helping someone is possible. There are always things we can do for one another. Nothing beats reaching out a hand when we can.

And now that I have hung this 500 word star in my sky, it is right back to the couch for me. Where, after an hour or so, I will have to fight off the voice in my head that will say, "You should get some work done."

And I will answer, "Are you *trying* to kill me?"

JUST SHOW UP

ONE OF LIFE'S UNAVOIDABLE responsibilities is to show up at your friend's fund-raising event.

You could just send a check. But if she has been reminding you of the date for months and cheerfully comparing her entertainment line-up to Broadway, you really do need to attend.

It all makes me think of a cop on *Law & Order* who put it like this: "Man, you just need to shut your yap and show your face, got it?"

I'm joking. But even so, I would never want to let her down. She has been a good friend. Loyal. Generous. Honest, but not too.

However.

I am a little fearful of round table seating. I feel like I am ten years old again waiting for the popular kids to reject me. I always try to find at least one person I can see myself making small talk with, since attending a fund-raising event alone is a little like attending a wedding alone. The once-overs can feel as obvious as the silent plea for checks to be written.

While gazing over the sea of strangers nosing their way through the tables and auction prizes like fish through coral, I spot one woman who looks interesting enough, presuming tree-of-life earrings imply someone would be fun to talk to. I put my coat over the back of the chair next to hers and we get to talking.

I wish I could say it is possible to recognize what side of an issue someone is on based on earrings alone, but one should never make such assumptions. We are only halfway through our arugula salads when her inquiries make my heart beat a little faster.

Granted, I am sensitive about immigration finger-pointing, I won't deny it; I feel protective. It has made me think seriously about what I will allow people to say in my presence.

The more my tablemate drank, the more probing she became. "Your family came legally, though. Right? They didn't come expecting a free ride."

My mind raced. *How many immigrants do you know who expect a free ride? Most come to work at kitchen or field labor. I am fairly certain you did not raise YOUR son to rush on down to Fresno to hand pick tomatoes. But to answer your question directly, no, my father's family did not come legally, they came desperately. I believe it is why they were called WOPS. Without Papers. I believe, mercifully, the legal process began after they arrived. Oh, and one other thing: May you never have to run for YOUR life.*

But I just sat there with a big fat frozen smile on my face, trying to be socially correct, where the worst thing you can say is the truest thing you feel. The polite thing to do is say, "Excuse me," and pretend to see someone you know across the room.

And what do you know? I do know someone. And she is seated at the head table.

On one of the rare occasions when my father told a story about "the war," there's one that still makes my knees go weak: After Mussolini sided with Hitler, his soldiers marched into my dad's village and, to assert their authority, they lined up all the families in the piazza and without warning, shot one mother, one father, and two children.

My sister and I talk a lot about how my dad remained perpetually fearful about so many things. And though that didn't make growing up under his roof any picnic, I now understand the reasons better. No one gets over seeing neighbors shot down like pigeons.

After congratulating my friend on a wonderful evening (it was, she raised a ton of money for her scholarship program), I passed a table where two women were discussing Good Friday, "What's so good about it again?" one said in an unabashed voice that could draw anyone in.

"It's when, you know, Jesus rose from the dead."

"Now *there's* an image that has served men well. Was it before or after he walked on water?" She laughed. "My first husband thought he could walk on water, too, but my lawyer showed him just how quickly you can go under."

Every once in a while, you hear someone who reminds you that it is possible to be irreverent, humble, and funny all at once. It was like meeting someone from my tribe.

Or the tribe I aspire to.

Not that it is *ever* smart to assume.

I pull up a chair anyway. "Mind?" I say.

I've replayed a lot of the evening over and over in my mind, looking for a reason I should have stayed home in my sweats, but I can't find one.

It was a good cause. I met some good people.

And the entertainment *was* top notch.

IMPOSSIBLE

WITH AFTERNOON SUNLIGHT pouring into the front seat of my car, I arrive in Port Angeles to teach a choreography class.

I've known the owner of the studio since she struggled with the idea of opening. Her journey has been like witnessing a beautiful becoming. She has the rare gift of real passion, and it's a great feeling when you can tell that someone who loves to teach has made it their lifework.

I adore her, as she knows.

It's been a long drive from Seattle. I'm eager to stretch but I am taken aback as soon as I'm inside the door.

A boy, maybe four years old, mimics every move, line, and position the girls in ballet class make. I feel as though I know his excitement as well as I know my own.

His mother, slouched in a chair, is lost in her phone. I look at the boy, at his mother, back at the boy. We both turn to look at the dancers. I tell him that I hope he takes ballet class, too, which prompts a sudden lift of mom's chin. I say what I am thinking anyway, "Boys make wonderful ballet dancers."

"Not in Port Angeles," she snaps back, sitting up straighter now, scorn clinging to her tone, as if ballet isn't something her son, or any real man, should get too close to.

The boy looks at me again, at his mom, at the floor. He jams his fist into the palm of his hand.

It's like watching a leaf wilt on the vine. I don't often use the word *crestfallen*, but I know it when I see it.

I've grown used to arriving in studios where I can feel as if *my* every move is not only visible but assessed. It's why I don't allow parents to watch my class. I want my students to relax. *I* want to relax. It's one benefit of being a master teacher, I set my own rules. And though feelings can run a little high as parents realize they really do have to leave, I have yet to find one director who doesn't support my request.

I had to say something more to the boy. It wasn't an overwhelming feeling, more of a swell in a larger sea of swells. "You are a natural born dancer," I said.

He smiled at me, stopping for a quick look at his mom who shifted slightly on her chair as if something (other than me) poked at her.

The truth, of course, is that all children are natural born dancers. It's only later that we learn to suppress the desire to move to the sounds we hear. I was impressionably young when my first dance teacher complimented my turn out, but I remember how good his praise felt and how motivated I was because of it. Never underestimate the importance of building confidence in a child, that's my teaching motto.

I also know what it means to simply accept what I am hired to do—teach a well-paced class—and I do this, with little want of anything in return but for every student to give it their best. But what happened that day is that the belief that only girls should dance pushed a little too many of my buttons. I had this overwhelming sense that bias would help shape this boy's future. He would be loved and well cared for, I could see that, but would he be allowed to become himself? Or be forced to explore his longings in secret.

There is magic inherent in a dance studio, in being surrounded by people who look as though they have found the one thing that makes them feel most alive. This is what the boy wanted for himself, I think, to move freely and enjoyably through space.

I also think he will have to learn to challenge himself in other ways, most likely on the ball field.

And I cannot know if playing ball will make him as happy as dancing seemed to make him. Anymore than I can know why his mother was so offended by it.

But if I let myself remember what stirred in this little boy to make him look so happy, what happened isn't hard to explain. I found his mother's reaction—to me, to what I said—asked of me something I found impossible to give: compliance.

Infidel

My last visit to a hair salon was a disaster. I wanted to throw off my robe and run out, refusing to pay, refusing to even look *back*.

When I arrived, the room seemed the same. The air reeked of Aveda, my magazine choices were still *People* and *House-Beautiful,* foil squares were still clamped to women's heads like barnacles to rock.

But I soon learned how *not* the same everything was.

Everyone knows that salons are all about the service, and by "service" I mean the scalp massage. I will tell you right now, a woman like me goes mostly for the massage. As soon as my head drops back, I get this giddy feeling that takes me back to when my sister Ginny used to wash my hair before setting it with Dippity-do, the two of us alone for once, the only two people in the world.

Now, I love my hairdresser, we get along like coffee and cream, but her assistant washes our hair. The good thing about this is that assistants are newly focused, extra careful and attentive. The bad part is that they still believe it is part of their job to ask a slew of questions, so it's harder to just close your eyes and pass out. After I shared the shortest possible answer about my line of work, I asked what she does, which, as soon as I said it, I knew how foolish it sounded since she was clearly *doing* what she does.

Only she was happy to tell me that she also coaches Christian volleyball.

I regarded those words thoughtfully for a moment.

I know it is fruitless to say certain things, to certain people, under certain circumstances, and I am *still* trying to figure out why knowing this only seems to make me speak faster. "What does that mean exactly?" I say. "That your players are Christian? Or that you only play Christian teams?"

"Both?" she said. But I don't think she meant it as a question.

I thought of the line: *Don't get so tolerant that you tolerate intolerance.* Which is why I had to go and say, "But wouldn't you learn more by playing all sorts of people who practice all types of religions and believe in all kinds of gods," I paused, "and goddesses?"

"There is only one God!" she snarled.

And I let her. I let her snarl at me.

Hairdressers are trained to steer the conversation away from politics and religion, so I wondered if the recent Supreme Court ruling about that homophobe-baker-of-wedding-cakes had empowered certain people. Including me.

"Well," I said. "That's like saying there is only one flavor of ice-cream."

I didn't plan on saying it. I just said it.

And right after I did, a trickle of water dribbled down my back, not enough to make any real difference, but I felt its deliberateness, there was no doubt in my mind that the dribble was deliberate.

And then a stream rushed down.

To get through the next few minutes, I tried thinking happier thoughts like bicycling through the Methow Valley, writing Mitch McConnell an angry email, eating miso butterfish at Shiro's Sushi, writing Mitch McConnell an angry email. IN ALL CAPS.

And then, you won't believe it, she pulled my hair. Not a gentle tug that sort of feels good, but a yank. As if to say, "Infidel!"

I shot up, spun around. I couldn't believe what she had done, I couldn't speak. We stared at each other. In the mirror, her eyes were cold, as if she struggled to contain all of the confusion she has about "non-believers," but quickly shifted into the self-satisfied look of someone who had just done something they really *enjoyed* doing.

I thought, "*Say* something! Why are you acting so cowardly?"

Asking myself the question helped, but answering it is what made me keep my mouth shut. *I am not acting cowardly. I am acting like an adult.*

And what saved me from the part of myself willing to go down swinging was another approach: *intolerance fails us all in the end.*

But to be honest, by then, I didn't know if I was being too tolerant or too *in*tolerant.

And as many times as I think about it now, I still don't know.

Silent Too Long

Unless it has happened to you, you'll probably never fully understand.

And that's okay.

My intention is not to persuade you, but to go back in time to a story that may be considered old news, but it is where my career life began, and it is still the oldest truth, and perhaps the most prevalent: why I believe women like Dr. Christine Blasey Ford.

In my quest to know their stories better, I think it is finally time to re-examine my own.

I was too young during the Anita Hill hearings to grasp how hard it must have been to describe, in clinical detail, the advances experienced from her employer. I'm sure she sensed—what with the cameras and the audience and the exhaustion—that the lines were beginning to blur in many people's minds. The humiliation of a come-on is difficult to convey even without all the theatrics, especially to those who still believe "boys will be boys" or that a man's advances *could* be considered a compliment. My own parents talked like this.

And when the Me Too Movement was abbreviated to a hashtag, I feared something about its effect would also be reduced. I did feel a responsive shift because of the movement, but it was Dr. Ford's story that finally budged me to speak.

I suppose my long delay stems from fears we have all heard: that people wouldn't believe me, that it would sound like sour grapes, that it was my fault since I *agreed* to meet one of my employers for lunch, another for a drink.

There is little I miss about writing for major media, but, so young at the time and desperate to have my work read, I allowed myself to make the naive assumption that "friendship" between all colleagues was possible. What is more intoxicating to a young writer than her employer showing interest in her work? It is one of our deepest human desires to have one's work be noticed. I was too inexperienced to realize how some employers seek out young writers who are willing to hand over their souls.

In my case, both men—one my editor at one of two major papers in our city at the time, and the other my producer at one of Seattle's NPR affiliate stations—gave me a great opportunity.

And both took it away.

Because they could.

One day I was writing for the paper, then I was not. One day I was airing my commentary for the station, the next I was not.

Years later, I got an email from the editor. He wrote how my stories "were some of the finest that ever crossed my desk" but said nothing about what happened. Was this his way of apologizing without having to say the words? Did he think I'd ever forget how enraged he became when I mentioned weekend plans with my husband? And how he glared at me and said with words not nearly as harsh as their tone, "You never said you were married."

"Why does it matter?" I said.

But in truth, I knew that it did matter. So I'd learned to slip silently between my professional and private life. Is there anything more demeaning than having to pretend that we are single in order to secure a job?

There is not.

I'm not the first woman to hide her married life for professional advancement, and I doubt I'll be the last. But I grew tired of hiding. And for weeks after he stopped accepting my work, it was a period of my life when disillusionment entered my mind so crushingly that all confidence left it.

Thinking back to that time, I was excited to move to a city again after having lived in a small town on the Olympic Peninsula. Living in Belltown where the whole messy mix of colorful humanity passed by, I was proud to write for a major paper that I could *walk* to; a radio station that I could bus to.

I did go on to write for another section of the paper. I thought it might be better for my career, and for my psyche, if I spent my time counting my blessings about this new opportunity and less time thinking about what had happened to me. Women learn to cope with certain humiliations. I thought my only choice was to be willing to learn *how*.

When I agreed to meet my radio producer for a drink "to talk about your future at the station," he rubbed his middle finger up and down the back of my hand. I pretended it was nothing. I brushed his hand away. He stopped returning my emails.

The worst part is that it was all just a game to these men.

I believe Dr. Ford because for the last fifteen years, I never told anyone, other than my husband. And, no, I can't remember the exact bar, or what I had to drink, and if I had to recall if there were other people around our table, I could not. It was a long time ago and I fear I'd stumble over the details. My strongest memory of that meeting was that it happened during a chapter in my life that had everything to do with setting goals and doing everything (but not *that*) I needed to do in order to reach those goals.

As the years passed, I let a small part of me forget what had happened.

Until the Kavanaugh hearings. Then I started telling everyone.

The first stranger I told was my LYFT driver. The same public radio station was on and I asked him to turn it off. When I told him why, he reached over to silence it and told me that his sister had been through the same ordeal where she worked.

I told my friend Stephanie the next day.

It seems I am forgiving these men finally, leaving the anger behind.

No, that's not quite true. It is *me* I am still trying to forgive.

For staying silent so long.

Safe, Sure, Free

A FEW YEARS BACK, for all the reasons we love to travel, I decided that each fall Larry and I would bicycle through countryside we've never seen. We both love long stretches of undeveloped land *and* wine-tasting, so the Willamette Valley in Oregon seemed like a good fit for us.

We began our trip in McMinnville, planning to ride south to Silverton, then North to Hood River. Right away we loved the landscape, which is good because we needed to ride through forty miles of it a day to reach our accommodations along the way.

About twenty miles outside of Silverton, we saw a handmade sign for farm-fresh eggs. Now, I can eat nearly a dozen eggs a day when I'm long-distance riding, so when the farmer scooped our eggs right from under cackling chickens, I was thrilled! His English wasn't great, and my Spanish is worse, so I decided that instead of asking him if he'd hard-boil them for an extra fee, I would ask the first woman I saw down the road. I imagined her working outside in her garden. Please-oh-please, I'd say.

And there she was, about a mile down the rural stretch of road, sitting in a white plastic chair by her mailbox, happy to say hello, happy to boil my eggs. Her husband shook my husband's hand, and off the two of them walked to sit in the garden, while she and I walked to the kitchen. I think they were just so happy to have someone, anyone, other than each other to talk to.

The eggs boiled. She talked and talked. Her whole life story. And I was happy to listen, remembering how lonely life can be when there isn't anyone to talk to.

When the eggs were done, she offered me a tour of the farm and I said sure, because the house, the garden, the chickens, it all looked so peaceful and bucolic, everything city life *isn't*. And they were such sweet, whole-hearted, generous, people. That's the way I saw them.

Until we got to the barn.

Now, just because someone wants to show you their "hobby" in the loft, doesn't mean you should scramble up the ladder to take a peek. I have no clear memory of climbing, just of what slowly came into view once I had. "Oh," I said. And quickly backed down the rungs.

As soon as I turned around, I could see that she was smiling. I wasn't surprised. Even with my back to her I knew that she was smiling.

I've seen that same smile on a lot of people lately. The way they laugh, pat each other on the back, shake each other's hands. You would think they were members of a bowling league instead of Congress.

In mind now, whenever I think of that loft, there is this to recall: swastikas in every size imaginable, the largest in the center of a huge red drape that trailed over the loft's edge as if out of a Nazi government window in 1933. Pictures of Obama, one with an arrow through his head, one with a bullet, one with a monkey's mouth and ears. And there were 14/88 stickers everywhere. If you have to look up what those numbers mean, so did I. Just be sure you are sitting down.

Larry said he could tell something was wrong by the look in my eyes. How fast we rode away. "Something awful happened," I said, soon as the farmhouse was out of view.

"What kind of awful?" he said.

Today, I don't think viewing racist propaganda was the worst thing that could have happened on our ride. My eyes are now more open to people who may seem like perfectly nice, live-and-let-live folks on the outside but are something completely different within.

Everything about first impressions has changed for me, *I* have changed.

Because it's one thing to hear about places that attract whole populations of haters like wintering birds. Quite another to meet two members of its flock.

If I had a picture of what my face must have looked like when I reached the top rung of the ladder, I'd put it on the fridge next to the picture of us posing on the Columbia River Bike Trail.

As we rode away, I had such a hollow feeling. It took about ten miles of cycling to shake it off.

Around sunset we were in awe of the natural world again, and I smiled watching the birds. I sat down next to Larry and he put his arm around my shoulders.

The birds made me happy because—I admit—I've always loved those scenes in a movie when a flock flies overhead at just the right moment to remind us how to feel safe, sure, free.

STUFF

THE OTHER DAY WHEN I WAS flipping through a magazine, a line jumped out at me: "We fall in love with objects not only for what they are, but for what they allow us to believe we will become."

It was three summers ago when I spotted a set of six vintage long-stem aperitif glasses at Seattle's Bigelow Block Sale. I picked one up, blew on it though it wasn't dusty, set it back down. I didn't want to seem *too* interested.

I continued to walk up and down Bigelow because, as any shopper knows, joy is in the pursuit, not in the prize.

Unless the prize is six vintage long-stem aperitif glasses that belong to a woman who wears a turquoise pendant, numerous turquoise rings, and her car has Arizona plates. What this meant to me was that maybe, just maybe, she was moving back to the desert and I'd get a really sweet deal.

The second time I passed the glasses, I knew I had to have them, a yearning I have little luck talking myself out of when it hits. And near the corner of Boston and Bigelow it hit hard.

The oddest thing about seeing the glasses is that during all the years I was actually looking for vintage long-stem aperitif glasses, I could never find one. Not at a rummage sale. Not at Goodwill. Not at Value Village. The only one I have ever sipped from had a shorter stem, and it came from a display cabinet in my mother-in-law's dining room, the cabinet that not only became the most cherished possession in my husband's family estate, but the one that his sisters are still fighting over. The last time my sister-in-law, Caren, talked about the cabinet, her lips quivered.

As I made my way down Bigelow, I was remembering some of the hurtful emails Caren and her sister sent back and forth over the cabinet (they cc'd in the siblings), when the glasses caught my eye for the third time. The way they gleamed felt like a sign—nothing smaller than a sign, anyway.

I walked closer.

My own mother had aperitif glasses, but I can't remember ever using them, and I have no idea what happened to them. But the memory of them brought back a whole stage of my girlhood. Suddenly I was no longer an adult. I was thirteen again and scribbling into a diary, "There was a new boy on the bus today and he is *sooo* cute."

When I finally decided to buy the glasses, the sale was slowing down, with some sellers folding up their tables already, but there were my unsold vintage glasses, flashing me smiles. I imagined that along with those smiles would be tête-à-têtes cozy and intimate, so many things to talk about.

I vowed to give one to each of my closest friends. But wait. Don't they keep telling me they need to down-size and move to god-knows-where? I'd never want to burden them with any more stuff.

And though *I* would never label a vintage long-stemmed aperitif glass "stuff," I know there is a personal fine line between treasure and tchotchke.

Besides, I'll need the entire set now that I have matured into someone who will serve an aperitif at her small, but suave get-togethers.

Even if this is Belltown, circa now, which must hold the record for the fewest vintage long-stemmed aperitif glasses ever.

But I'm okay with that.

I have become.

A Prime Reminder

Whenever I walk from Belltown to South Lake Union, I leave one Seattle to enter another.

The dividing line begins on Sixth Avenue. It's abrupt. We are forced to accept it.

Like Big Tech, there is no other way to think of Seattle now without thinking Big Amazon. Big Amazon is the BIG of our era. No one thinks of Boeing anymore. I don't even think they think of Microsoft. Bill and Melinda? Who are they?

Even more surprising is how much quieter it has become in Belltown. Some people might say ghostly quiet. It tries and tries, but something always keeps it from full-scale gentrification.

The drug dealers are back in droves, that might be why. There is a lot of money to be made from a lonely, far-from-home workforce and as my neighbor Marlin put it, "dealers are no dummies."

Actually, I don't remember the dealers ever being gone. They just used to hide in the shadows more. Or maybe I just imagined they did.

Still, I try not to think of Big Amazon as the king of all kings. I don't want to worship that crown. And what makes me want to say this right now is that I was shopping at Whole Foods this morning and there they were, trying to make their way into my cart: crisp Fuji apples on sale.

The produce department makes everything look so bucolic and inviting and unrestricted that I didn't think I *had* to be a Prime member. I can even become unpleasant in the face of that question.

But as soon as I placed my apples on the conveyor belt, I was instantly reminded of the aggressive nature of Big Membership: I could forfeit my apples or pay double.

A stone fell from my heart.

Not a stone. A rotten Fuji apple.

It's always been easier to manipulate people into believing that they are being rewarded, rather than actually reward them, equally. It's also effective, or Whole Foods wouldn't be the most expensive grocery store in America and one of the most crowded.

The whole idea of Prime membership reminds me of a certain realtor I know. Getting rich beyond her wildest dreams, she is not about to apologize for any of it. She is also arrogant even at the Post Office, and most of the time I just want to pretend I don't see her.

I thought about toppling the display of apples on my way out of the store.

But here's the thing, I can *walk* to Whole foods. So, I pretend the convenience is enough because there are days it has to be enough. This is what I tell myself when I shop there so I can forgive them. Proximity is why I'm willing to tolerate their country-cozy propaganda that says, "c'mon, folks, we are free, open, classless" and then deliver the hard truth of social status as soon as we are inside the door: Membership is not only better *for* you. Members are better *than* you.

Fortunately, there are still a few humble buildings left downtown, erected long before the blocks-that-Amazon-built, if you take the time to look, and I like to take the time to look. And once I do, I realize how difficult it is to fully appreciate the cleverness of another era's marketing strategies until it has passed.

Take the Super Elephant Car Wash sign that revolves over Battery Street. When you think about it, its survival is a miracle. Even the elephant seems surprised to still be around. I appreciate it for reminding me of a previous time when there are few reminders left.

And the red-brick row houses on Third & Vine, built when a lot of Belltown still looked like this, a pocket of history that seems so quaint now that if I'm riding my bike and keep looking at the low buildings, I know that I'm going to hit the curb or a pedestrian, but I keep looking anyway because I not only want to grasp a time when architecture was considered the highest art form, I want to *feel* it. Before every trace of it comes down.

Because Big Whatever tends to erase history. Each new luxury-condo trendier than the last.

For weeks I carried a magazine around in my bag until I had the time to read a piece that compares development in present day Seattle to the Cultural Revolution in China where the hierarchy "robbed an entire generation of the concept of sentimental value."

Another point made was that a city, like a person, becomes what it rewards.

The Italians at the Aquarium

I AM REMINDED THAT I WAS not born on the West Coast by every conversation I have with someone who was.

Almost immediately, I am possessed by my East Coast self.

More to the point, my East Coast *Italian* self, different in attitude, tone, and temperament in ways I didn't fully understand when I was younger.

After years and years of trying, I still find it difficult to explain why Italians communicate the way we do, especially to people unaccustomed to passionate debate as a way to enjoy themselves.

Instead of lessening with time, the difficulty only increases.

I think it's because I weigh my words more carefully now, so as not to offend, since that's what I learned to do as soon as I started to make friends here, *weigh my words more carefully, so as not to offend.*

More difficult to explain are the emotional effects of this kind of quieter, less animated way of conversing on someone like me. I just don't feel like I am being *honest.* I long for conversations with more heat and hand waving. Anything less feels like withholding the truest I have to give.

The first time I had dinner at my in-law's table, I was afraid to open my mouth. I had no idea how to speak softly about things I read in the newspaper. I was shocked to sit with people, *intoxicated* people, who seemed to be content in the shoals of current events. The dining table of my youth was a competitive place. Everyone talked at once, interrupted each other, said things someone took offense to on purpose.

What fun!

And, of course, there is the matter of volume. Our neighbors, the McKenzie's, grumbled about how noisy we were especially on holidays when the uncles played poker, the aunts fought over food prep, all of the adults and a few of the cousins got drunk on homemade wine, our voices echoing louder and louder.

An Italian friend and I laugh about how this coast seems to have no limits on how many "likes" a person can squeeze into a sentence, or how many apologies, but just how loud we can speak or how close we can stand to each other when we do feels absolutely *firm*. It took only a few days in this city for me to realize that personal space was really a thing. *Spazio personale?* What on earth?

People often say that Italians are just more "in touch" with our feelings, though my husband would probably say overly so. Like how he once made fun of how flushed my cheeks get when I'm angry (or extremely happy or even the slightest bit drunk) by calling me "hot-faced," even if he hasn't dared call me that to my hot face ever since. Or the way he replies, "don't drive yourself crazy." Like, say, we're having friends over and I begin to worry that maybe we should have bought white wine instead of only red. "Mary Lou, there's plenty of wine, don't drive yourself crazy." And there is a moment, maybe two, before he pulls on his shoes and goes for the white.

All of this comes to me now because the other day I walked to the aquarium after reading *The Soul of An Octopus.* (I poured myself into those pages. Every once in a while you find a book that lets you feel every good feeling at once.)

But to my surprise, it wasn't the octopus I wound up studying. It was a group of Italians.

And yes I heard them before I saw them. If that is what you are wondering.

Most days I trust there are intentional coincidences, and I believe this one occurred to remind me of a huge part of my personality I neglect now that I (try to) live by a different code of ethics. Or what I jokingly call (but only to East Coast friends) BIDAN: *Bring it down a notch.* Just so I won't yell, "I'm not stressed, people, I'm excited! There's a difference!" at the top of my lungs just about each and every day I live here.

Watching the group talk and touch and embrace each other freely, I never felt more distant from the city in which I reside.

If the desire to be in the company of your tribe is one of the most overwhelming of human connections, I was quickly reminded of where my qualities and personality traits originate. I could see why I wave my hands around a certain way and touch people when we chat because this is how communication has always been done. I felt an urge to run up to them and say, "I'm Italian, too!"

Thankfully, I stopped myself.

I followed them into the undersea dome, though.

And I wanted to hug them. With my whole body. This is another mid-life change that has come over me: When I want something, my longing doesn't seem to come from a single driven desire inside my head, but from my every bone and nerve. Even my skin seems to want what it wants. *Pronto!*

I think this has always been a part of my nature, it's just more pronounced now.

I wanted to hold on to this family with such a strong intensity that when I couldn't, I walked past them feeling deprived, devastated, *deflated.*

I called my friend Stephanie. She wasn't born in Seattle, but she feels at home here.

She had no idea why I was calling, and I didn't bother to say, but her greetings are always warm, and as soon as I heard her voice, I felt grounded.

That might be an overstatement.

I felt *more* grounded.

LISA'S 50TH

I CAN STILL SEE THE BLACK SMUDGE of mascara under Mali's eyes, and nothing revives me more than laughter-tears. They expose why coming together, in person, is so important.

But like a lot of writers, I have to work at my social skills. They weren't the best when I was a younger writer. And they still aren't. I easily fall victim to one of the less talked about truths about being a capable writer: I am a bit *in*capable in the real world.

Eventually, I relax. With maybe a menu in one hand, a glass of wine in the other. Like this, I'm at my best. And when six of us met to celebrate our friend Lisa's fiftieth birthday, if there was one moment when I saw clearly why, it was when I looked around our table.

I was blown away by the sight of us.

Generous, multifarious *us*.

Mali is from Thailand. Our first conversation was a turning point in my life. There is a lot to learn from the Thai concept of *sanuk* which is often explained as fun, but it's so much more than fun. It's about seeking joyful satisfaction from every place, everyone, everything. *I have lessons to learn*, I thought.

Ly was born in Vietnam. She came to Seattle eleven years ago with little money and a wellspring of hope, eager to open a nail salon. Today, she supports her parents and owns a home. No one emphasizes the words, *it's not how you make your money, it's how you save it* more than Ly. Things changed about a few of the wasteful ways I spent money after we met. (I haven't told her that I have resumed manicuring my own nails.)

Lisa is third-generation Sonoma County Californian. She's our portal into vineyards and wineries and we gladly follow along. (The only following along with Lisa I have ever regretted is the Brazilian wax I did *not* want. "I don't think pubic hair needs to go the way of analog, do you?" I argued. Oh, the pain.)

Naturally more informed about wine than the rest of us, Lisa cannot be hurried through the wine list. She studies it like it is of great importance, causing us to wait edgily and think, *Lisa! Order a bottle already!* Yet when you take away our impatience, her choice continuously reminds us that wine can be a luscious experience. "Now, *this* is good wine," we wind up saying. When she assesses a Pinot Noir, I want to *be* Pinot Noir. I want to have balance and character and forwardness, too.

Romy is a schoolteacher from Zimbabwe. Whenever she tells a story, whether it's about family, food, or her village, there is no going back to how I once thought about family, food, or village life. I think this is what teaching is, to open minds. Plus, she's really hopeful and positive about national politics. Much more hopeful and positive than I am.

Chris is the only one of us born in Seattle. She is only first generation, her parents are from Austria, but she calls herself a local yokel, though *we* know not to call her that. She pulled up to Ray's Cafe on a Honda motorcycle wearing a black leather jacket. Her boots and jeans are also black, but on Chris "biker" looks easygoing, unaffected. She is comfortable in her own skin like no other friend of mine. Honestly, a lot of my friends are more of an uptight bunch compared to Chris.

My parents are not from Sonoma wine-making country. Our wine was made in a cold dark cellar with creepy-crawlies everywhere. I've since learned that it *is* possible to like cheap Italian wine. It has other possibilities. Like soup stock. Or you can bake it into a chocolate cake.

I look around our birthday table and think how everything about being an immigrant today is not so different than in my parent's day. Their struggles have always been harsh.

I'll end by saying what I hope for all of us, that we remember to say a simple "thank-you" to all of the hard-working people we see around us every day, who risk everything in order to work, save, survive.

Khaawp khun.

Cảm ơn bạn.

Hey, thanks.

Waita hako.

Thank you so much. I really appreciate it.

Ciao grazie.

Lyft Share, Yes Please

Not only are some of my worst days the ones when I think driving across town is a good idea, but with the Lyft share option, I can no longer justify owning a car.

One friend says that I'm more "cut out" for public transit. Whatever that means. "But I'm from Seattle," she said.

"But Seattle is very forward-thinking about transportation," I said.

I don't remember much else about that conversation, just that the real differences between us were highlighted in the collection of mirrors above the bar at Tavolàta where they've been brought to light before. Last time she said that my apartment reminds her of a bento box. I left her thinking *patience, Mary Lou, patience is key.*

Granted, I live in Belltown, where parking is more of an issue. But the fact that I can ride to just about anywhere I need to go for under five dollars if I'm willing to share feels like a gift.

It is a gift. "Thank you!" I cried the first time I tapped the share option, as though I'd just unwrapped one.

One problem I foresee, because I work in Everett once a month, is dreading the long bus ride north.

But staring out the window still sounds better than driving I-5 where the moment I have to make my way over to the exit lane immediately turns reality into a full-blown-blasphemous ordeal. Luckily, as far as I know, swear words have never made anyone crash into an oncoming car.

Still, closeness on a bus does *not* feel like a gift. Closeness on a bus feels like its greatest downside. I don't know why there is such a difference. I wonder about it. I like talking to people in a car, but on the bus, I deflect most exchanges. And I know this sounds partial, prejudice, or whatever, but my imagination (that is seldom politically correct) thinks "3-D" describes my bus-riding days. Disheartening. Dismal. Does he even know how bad he smells?

By contrast, I rarely leave my Lyft in a deeper state of detachment. Lyft drivers can be surprisingly enlightening. It's not hard to break through. My last driver was from Afghanistan. He wanted to know all about Velocity, the dance studio he was driving me to because he loves to dance—but under the Taliban was not allowed to. He had a regal presence with dark hair and eyes and a white dress shirt. I wore workout sweats. But I felt less frumpy as soon as we picked up another rider who was covered with dog hair and what looked like dog slobber.

He was nice though.

And we got to talking. Like airplane chumminess, it's difficult to refuse.

After we dropped him off, our driver said he was grateful to be in this country. "I wish Americans had just *helped* us, not invaded." I found his comment refreshing. I no longer want to hear what journalists and pundits think Afghans think. I want to hear from Afghans what they think.

We talked about the last mass shooting though, sadly, I don't even remember which one. He said—I'm paraphrasing, but only slightly— "he had so many rounds, that crazy shooter! He shot and shot! I don't think our forefathers had an AK-47 in mind when they thought about the right to bear arms. They never meant *that*."

What really got me was the way he said, "our" forefathers. I mean, every time our government makes me angry, I'm more than happy to call myself Italian again.

Not every ride is as interesting. One driver picked me up at the Fauntleroy Ferry and for the entire drive I was on the receiving end of a nonsensical monologue. Before driving off, he thanked me for the great conversation. "Is that what that was?" I said and slammed the door.

And when I'm in for the day, not going anywhere, and hear a car pull up in front of my building and then the well-mannered accent of a driver asking the rider's name, often I'll get up from my desk and look out the window and think, that driver, in his grey Toyota Prius, who *is* he?

GOOD TASTE

THERE MUST HAVE BEEN a precise time in foodie consciousness when eating became not only what we do, but what we hope to *experience*.

I'm sure I've read in one of Ruth Reichl's books the exact date, restaurant, and chef that changed everything about eating in this country. This would have been the same date that changed everything for women like my mother whose pasta would please any palate but was still more likely to be called *macaroni*.

But not picturesque macaroni, like a *Bon Appétit* image—flawlessly wound linguini on a spotless white platter. Our family's floral serving bowl had a chipped edge and sauce dripped over its rim. Its purpose had less to do with presentation and more to do with volume. We crossed ourselves, said a prayer, and dug in.

And never once did we think of ourselves as "food people." Food was simple, respected, *ex*pected. Nor did we compliment it or, regrettably, my mother.

On no occasion did we eat at a restaurant.

This is so different from how a lot of my Seattle friends grew up, especially those originally from California, who talk about dining out once a week at their family's favorite eatery and are comfortable with words like *infusion* and *plated*. Growing up near the first food scenes of Berkeley and Napa, food became something to intellectualize, appraise, shake your head at. Or nod.

And why I reluctantly eat out with them.

And when I say reluctantly, I mean I am filled with anxiety at the very thought.

Foodie-behavior embarrasses me. More frankly, I find people who need to tell the waiter how much they know about the food insufferable. I grow impatient with how long it takes a foodie to study the menu, and don't even get me started on the wine list. Their questions can sound more like interrogations that, to me, hijack the intention of sharing a meal—where *our* questions to *each other* are the point, or should be.

Years ago, I went to our city's landmark fervent-fine-dining destination, Canlis, to see what all the fuss was about. The food was exquisite, the service impeccable, but my friend Shanta and I couldn't stop giggling at the absurdity of it all, the extravagance.

Clearly, under my white collar, I'm hopelessly blue.

Unlike my parents, I can appreciate, even afford, a place like Canlis now and again, but I will never feel comfortable eating in such a place.

Not as comfortable as, say, my friend Gina. I love to listen to her talk about food. She is an original life-is-all-about-eating-in-the-finest-restaurants example, the only person I've ever met who admits, flat out, she has never had to work. Seriously, she calls work "the four-letter word." Dining out is her work. And she does it well. If she recommends a restaurant, you know the food will be *an experience.*

My friend Lena, who was my college roommate (so perhaps we are still a wee bit competitive), moved to Sonoma and last year we had a huge row at the sort of restaurant where even if you skip the starter and desert you are going to drop a couple hundred bucks, and that's if you stick to one glass of wine.

Unwisely, I had two.

Two is where insecurities can quickly transgress.

The waiter returned to our table four times to take Lena's wine order. At one point I had this vision that long after the entire staff had gone home, here would be Lena, still inspecting the vintage and pedigree while the new light of dawn filled the dining room. Finally, I screamed, "Oh my god, Lena! Is this what moving to Sonoma does to a girl from Erie, Pennsylvania?"

Immediately I felt so bad tears sprang to my eyes and all I could do is cross my arms tightly and rock back and forth a few times. I think she has somewhat-basical-ly forgiven me for being such an ass.

I've yet to forgive myself, though.

More recently my friend Sara (who in our circle isn't a foodie, she's *the* foodie), called me out on my impa-tience. "Why do you get so impatient when I ask the waiter questions?"

For weeks, I didn't know how to explain my bad manners because I wasn't clear about their origin.

What *is* this all about?

I have this nagging suspicion that I see, or want to see, myself as my family sees themselves: hardworking, unpretentious, unimpressed by prestige, status, or distinction. It secures me to myself, to my past, to everything I believe in, possibly to earth. And all the foodie talk—no matter how delicious the food or how beautifully it's *plated*—unravels me.

Until I am reminded of Aristotle's advice, "It is the mark of an educated mind to be able to entertain a thought without accepting it."

For several minutes I let those words seep in.

I believe the man had good taste.

Pun intended.

Why It Remains

AT FIRST, IT WAS JUST ANOTHER upsetting truth to hear. Maybe a little worse than all the other upsetting truths of the day, but I was trying to stay calm.

But if you must *try* and stay calm, you are not calm. It's more likely that you are already deeply upset, trying hard to not have a total meltdown.

It took me another minute to admit that I was not only upset, I was afraid. And from the feel of the ire rising in me, furious.

I won't say her name, only that she is twenty-three, strong, a ballet dancer. "I had an earache," she said. "A bacterial infection. My doctor prescribed an antibiotic. Then he wrote another prescription."

"For what?" I asked, sensing she didn't want to say.

"Oxycodone."

And that—*that*—is why I am furious.

"No," I said. Do not take that. Take aspirin," I insisted. Strange what stays in the memory. I remember thinking how grateful I was to know she was the kind of friend I could say that to.

The next day she was fine. "I took a couple of aspirin until the eardrops kicked in."

Maybe it's because of the way our streets and parks and underpasses look, the degradation so blatant, our whole city reduced to three words: *the homeless problem*— that made this prescription seem different from all the other over-prescribing I've heard about. And I know exactly why: I love my friend. I want to protect her, watch over her, shield her.

Last week, I had dinner with a friend who lives in West Seattle. She arrived flustered because just before driving to Belltown, there was a shootout in front of her house. "A shoot out!" she cried. "And there's a new homeless camp I can see from my living room window. Apparently, the drug-dealers have come to prey on them." She is seriously thinking of moving out of the city.

I said how I *used* to feel grateful that our local news wasn't all about who shot who and why. We discussed how we believe the homeless "problem" is more of an addiction and lack of mental health services *result*. "I'm beginning to believe that Seattle is one big social experiment gone terribly wrong," she said.

And I was so upset, I said, "If I hear one more thing about affordable housing. What kind of housing can an addict afford? I will tell you what kind. It's called a tarp." (This was after I had a dream, a *nightmare*, that I was living under a tarp behind Bethany Presbyterian Church, proving the closer we get to what truly terrifies us, the deeper we try to bury it.)

Talk about a nightmare. All this makes me think of Antonio. Antonio has worked for years at Assagio's on 4th Avenue, our neighborhood Italian restaurant. The food isn't great, I'm not sure it ever was, but the cocktails are, and the owner flirts like crazy with every woman who walks through the door. Which we love.

My point is—the horrible *truth* is—that it was Antonio's wife who was working the front desk in the chiropractor's office in Burien when a stray bullet hit and killed her. I still don't know how to process this, let alone imagine how Antonio copes. When I think of him, I crumble inside.

And just the other day my husband was at the US Passport office downtown fifteen minutes before it opened. He took a seat on the granite steps, right across from two young men. "Just kids, really," he said. "I assumed they were homeless by their torn clothing, filthy backpacks, and shared Colt 45 quart of beer. But what really got me was their street tips."

I sat on the couch, immobilized, listening to what he overheard: Which condo lobbies are the easiest to break into. How the library's new landscaping is no longer a good place to hide your backpack for a few hours when you need to get high. Which public parks lock the bathroom doors at sunset.

I became even more incensed, which is a Seattle way of saying that I am so pissed off that I could scream bloody murder at the raging greed on the part of pharmaceutical companies and doctors who still pump out opiate prescriptions just because.

And by *because*, I mean *because of the profits*.

I know that I am not a medical expert and that the world of health care changes constantly. But when the newest upsetting truth lands right in front of me, it's like a warning to make sure I see what is going on.

And this is what I see: Money is made one addict at a time.

The Hurdle

Several times over the last few years, I've come face to face with the question: Should I at least *try* to help?

But really, who's to say it's for any of us to try and help someone who has not asked for our help. Maybe we should just go about our business and pretend nothing is wrong. Overlook it. Move on. Act as if someone we love *isn't* drinking too much.

I am trying really hard not to say what I'm thinking here: She is not just drinking too much. She is drinking until she is sloshed, soused, *blotto*. On a regular basis.

Our last dinner together, she couldn't focus. When she arrived, her words slurred together. She didn't eat what she ordered. Maybe a tiny bite. Not enough to sate a wren.

But it doesn't really concern me. Does it?

Honestly, I sometimes wish I *could* be this unaffected. I really do.

This concern feels much more complicated than I can easily express, but the reason I'm going to try is that the whole hurdle can feel like holding on to the biggest white elephant. And I need to let go of the elephant.

That, and the fact that the number of times this has happened has increased over the years, while my knack for how to handle it has not.

I hadn't known in the beginning how serious my friend's drinking was, so I thought nothing of asking her to join me at the Black Bottle because it's within walking distance of her condo on 2nd and mine on 5th.

But half a dozen times now I've been in her company when she disrupts everything, and things suddenly feel as trying as I ever want them to be. My voice becomes deliberately more measured when she orders yet another drink and the waiter raises his eyebrows at *me*. And the question on everyone's mind becomes, "Is she all right? Should one of us walk her home?" These are not questions that generally occur at our dinners. Not in my circles anyway.

I know I am afraid to have The Conversation with her because you never know if the person will react by thinking, *now there's a good friend.* Or the exact opposite.

I believe we should approach our relationships with caring acceptance. But what about *concerned* acceptance? In *The Art of Loving*, the author says, "Nothing, especially love, can be mastered without practice, and practice involves discipline, patience, and supreme *concern.*"

Recently, I met a behavioral therapist, Rhonda, a friend of a friend. I wasted no time in sharing my concern-question with her. "Oh, you'd be surprised how many people who swear they only drink casually are full-blown alcoholics," she said.

I was somewhat-kind-of-fairly-certain she was talking about me. Until even something as simple as enjoying a glass of wine at the end of the day becomes a self-examination of hypocrisy.

Am I drinking too much?

To some it would seem so. Yes.

But come on, there is a difference between a glass of wine, maybe two if it's a weekend, and drinking until your eyes, your whole face, looks ready to drop.

I know this.

And yet, my thoughts cast doubt on my sauvignon blanc until I wind up pouring the last few swallows down the drain.

Once I'd got it in my head to try to help my friend, Rhonda warned me how tricky the conversation can be. She even emailed me a set of guidelines I followed to a tee.

I practiced what I was going to say beforehand.

I tried to pick the right time and place. Lunch at noon instead of a bar at six.

When we met, I didn't go so far as to touch my friend's arm, but I spoke gently. I kept to positive, supportive words. I avoided using "I" statements. Sort of.

I let her know I was worried. (*Is this a bad "I" statement? Or a supportive one?* I wondered.)

I braced myself for a negative reaction.

And I got one. Her reply felt like the worst cliché at a time like this. "I don't really have a problem. It's been a stressful time, that's all."

My insides dropped down a long shoot. And let me tell you, what she said next made me want to take off running.

"Maybe *you* have a problem, but I don't have a problem."

I tried not to take it personally.

I can accept failure. I can't accept not trying.

I really appreciate what this means now.

SORRY, TOM

I WROTE THIS STORY IN 2019 when our worries were ones we were more used to.

At the time, I don't remember consciously anticipating the Pride Parade. Not for any one reason, I've always enjoyed the parade—god, it's the best parade in the city—but it was just another thing about to happen, that's all, a fun pause in my weekend filled with proud people in great costuming.

I suppose this is how optimism works—you think if things are humming along smoothly they will keep humming along smoothly.

But there you go.

None of us knew that this year's parade would be cancelled or could have dreamed in our worst night terrors how unrecognizable the world would become overnight. None of us were prepared to worry about friends and family who got sick, understanding a pandemic, or surreal things like being afraid to hug people.

I had simply wanted to extend an apology to Tom Douglas after I offended two of his customers—and to be clear, I offended them on purpose. And this was before he had to close his restaurants, which doesn't even begin to cover how much sorrier this makes me, *beyond* sorry.

Today, I am nostalgic—deeply—for Seattle as it was that day.

≈

Many times in my life I have longed for the ability of turning a blind eye. Count to ten, focus on your breath, take time to process what you want to say—except not one of these silent approaches seems to work for me when I'm really mad. And no one can accuse me of looking the other way when I am really mad. If they could, I would never have allowed myself to say, "Hey! He's a friend of mine. Don't you dare say that about him!"

It was a lie. I didn't know the man walking by our tables wearing tighty-whities and a cowboy hat embellished with the colorful stripes of the rainbow flag, exactly what one would expect the day before our 45th Annual Pride Parade. LGBTQ's of every stripe were pouring into the city for the weekend festivities. Rainbow banners garlanded most doorways. It seemed to me nearly all businesses were proudly, peacefully on board.

Even the Rainier Club waived a banner over its entrance. I keep thinking how difficult it must have been to get some of the more senior members on board for *that*. Just to be invited behind those thick-brick walls, I had to be vetted. The programmer called it "a luncheon to get to know one another" but she would say that. (I changed three times, slightly different versions of pants and blouse that passed the only rule of professional dress I know: smooth top, hard bottom.)

I was just starting into my roasted tomato soup when the man at the next table said at the top of his voice, "Look at that freak!" And from his wife, "I can't believe they let people like that wander the streets."

I was so startled I almost dropped my spoon. That our city's public pride had turned into their private jeer, well, this kind of remark has always made me angry. Even as a kid. I loathe it even more today. Let us remember it wasn't made in a bar somewhere in Garfield County, but in Lola's restaurant on 4th Avenue. But narrow-mindedness knows no boundaries, it lives everywhere. I thought, *you can't let them say that!* And then, *here you go again, getting into trouble.* Next, *well, no one is perfect.*

I thought of my friend Dennis. He boasted tighty-whities in San Francisco's Castro Parade. Tighty-whities are a coming out thing. What a good man Dennis is. He makes me brave enough to speak up.

But before I said what I said, I asked the couple what I believed I already knew: that they were waiting for their cruise ship to leave in the morning. "Yes," they said in unison, off to Alaska from Missouri.

I worry when I see certain tourists walking in Belltown, though the reason has changed. I no longer warn them about walking on 3rd Avenue on their way to the Space Needle. Lately, I feel the opposite of protective for some of these inlanders—and this couple seemed even more out of place than most—I feel afraid.

Not for them, *of.*

Tom, I didn't set out to insult your customers by picking up my phone and speaking in a voice that was perhaps a bit louder than I'd intended. But their heartlessness egged me on. So, I went on. "I'm sitting here next to Tweedledee and Tweedledum-dum-dum-dum."

Even to me it sounded mean. *But how mean is mean enough?* (I can only hope that Elijah Cummings is smiling down on me. His whole life was about changing the world for the better. He helped integrate a segregated Baltimore swimming pool when he was 11 years old!) The couple shot me a surprised look, and lord knows what they mumbled to each other.

I'm not exactly mad at myself. Still, what I hope for next time is that I just shake my head and soldier on, silently.

Which is all fine and good if you are a soldier. Or prone to silence.

I was still questioning my behavior—I've had a lot of practice questioning—when I stood to go. The cowboy was sitting across the street at the Dahlia Bakery. I looked at him and thought, *I wish I didn't question myself as much. I wish I had half the self-confidence you seem to have.*

Back on the sidewalk, in direct contrast to any dum-dum disapproval, Seattle sparkled with irreverent acceptance.

And I loved us for it.

An Extraordinary Stage

I'm sitting down today to write about Elliott Bay Book Company.

I've written about so many things since *except* what happened to me the last time I read there, resisting because it can feel like too small a concern when you consider all that is happening in the world.

Though I am happy to escape all that is happening in the world.

Because when you have fallen into the pit of cable news, you have to question everything about it except your power to escape it.

Deep breath . . .

Not only has Elliott Bay Book Company been serving readers in our city for nearly fifty years, but it also has a long history of hosting authors. I believe its iconic stage is an extraordinary one that has an almost magical effect on the listening process.

Books bring us together in unexpected ways. When I gave my first reading at Elliott Bay, I watched two friends sit down next to each other and begin a courtship. Tender things can happen at a reading.

But tough things can happen, too. And at my last Elliott Bay reading, one of the toughest things for an author *did* happen.

And it keeps haunting me. Sigh.

My saving grace will be to keep to brief sentences. That way, maybe the memory won't trickle down my back in another cold sweat.

The man who stood to say that he didn't like my book *at all* shall remain anonymous.

His comment reached me before he came into view.

I felt everything good I had said leave the room, the words growing small and faraway.

I noticed the dust balls on the floor underneath the first row of chairs.

I thought, *I know this guy.* This worried me.

A few years back the same man came to my reading at Town Hall Seattle. His criticism of my work that evening startled me in a way I hadn't known before. I'd never had to swallow such a strong dose of it in front of an audience, trying not to let it show.

Embarrassment can take over your expression if you are not prepared for a remark meant to take you down a notch. I remember seeing this look on an author's face back when Elliott Bay was still in Pioneer Square. She stood blinking and dumbfounded, like she wanted to say, "what is *wrong* with you?"

Now *I* wanted to say, "what is wrong with you?"

Mercifully, there was someone in the second row (I'm just going to admit that she is an avid reader of mine) who turned around and asked the man, "Why are you here?" Her will was stronger than his. What everyone, but everyone, heard was that.

You gain a sense about your audience, how you feel either connected to or removed from certain listeners. You notice things. And what I noticed was how the man seemed to be enjoying the attention. In fact, his smirk looked like the smirk of a man trying to *contain* all of the enjoyment he felt. *Shut up*, I thought. *Shut up*!

To quote my friend Ken Lambertson, "A public spotlight is a hard glare." And people show themselves in it in different ways. Sometimes they don't know how to phrase their question, so they grasp at straws. Or they can forget to ask one and tell a story instead. There is a silence to fill. So they fill it.

And every once in a while, there is someone who wants to fill it with malice.

I will always equate a reading with giving the best I have and receiving the best consideration in return. I still want that feeling for myself.

But I will always remember my last event at Elliott Bay as *the* reading where I realized there is absolutely no way, despite our best efforts, to plan for some surprises. We can never assume we won't face a heckler due to careful preparation.

When we are most vulnerable—and I'm certain this is why the man chose the public venues he did—there is only one thing we can do: keep going and never lose faith in the literary tradition we are honored to be a part of.

This has been behind me since October, when large audiences—a lump forms in my throat—were still gathering.

I just needed to see my way through it again.

I needed to get back up on that stage as quickly as the most rattled, flustered part of me could go.

Too Late to Hide

I'm afraid I was one of the "selfish Seattle people" who went outside to take in, *breathe* in, that glorious sunny Saturday back in March.

I dressed quickly, never taking my eyes off the light of day, moving in a different direction than the one I was supposed to follow. Like everyone, I was fraught, and these feelings drove me out the door, onto the streets, which seemed less unsafe than the stress within the walls of my home.

I solemnly pledged to keep my social distance.

There is something about the earliest days of spring, the increased sunlight, the balminess, it's invigorating. It makes everything about life feel *good*.

No matter how bad the news is.

No matter if my sister, a nurse in New York City, tested positive and needed an inhaler, antibiotics, and steroids to breathe without difficulty.

She is fine now. But we worried. Oh, how we worried.

For one thing, she had Rheumatic fever as a child. For another, she's been a smoker. The wine is poured, the cigarette is lit. The conversation intensifies, the next cig is lit. And so on and so on. For as far back as I can remember.

Before she got sick, we poo-pooed the hysteria. We called Corona "a new chew toy for the media." We compared our nation's numbers as if they proved something: 30,000 dead annually of flu viruses. 68,000 dead of opioid overdoses last year. 15,000 dead by gunshot. More than 32 million people worldwide with AIDS have died since the start of that epidemic. "And did you know?" I said, "that in the U.S., about 655,000 people die of heart disease each year? That *has* to have something to do with it." Said how we, together, were the perfect-storm of epi-centers: "You live in New York. I live in Seattle. We're *Italian*. We'll be shunned."

And when Larry said, "We can't stop living because we are afraid of dying," I grabbed onto his words like a sign. As if there had to *be* a sign. Of something. Encouraging. Soon.

I think the funniest thing I said to my sister (when we were still laughing) is what I said after she cried, "You would *think* I'd be more afraid of the virus. But I'm more afraid of the men running this country." And I said, "You would *think* there is a correlation between sheltering-in-place and sex, but there is not."

We said these things. We *meant* these things. We didn't know what was true. I don't trust the 24-hour news cycle and I've never been good at groupthink. We felt it was our duty to question everything. It *is* our duty to question everything. Accountability is the fundamental root of our democracy—or it will be again. Soon.

With any luck.

But when my sister had serious trouble breathing, like the streets around us, our doubts grew increasingly silent and empty.

So when the sun finally came out, *I* had to get out. Fresh air is my best strategy for coping with worry, and as soon as I was outside, my body started to relax. I crossed through Seattle Center and hiked up to Queen Anne until I found what I was looking for: earth.

Lush, leafy, irresistible, earth.

"You can't know how good it feels to get out of my condo!" I shouted to the first man I saw standing in his yard.

"Yes, I can," he said in a tone that convinced me condo-living was a subject he knew well. "I used to live in a condo." His smile was warm, as if we were old friends. It was all I could do not to walk closer. "I was board president for a while. But there is always someone who is trying to *oust* the board president. Most people were perfectly nice. Even the ousters were perfectly nice," he paused, "to my face."

I felt like I was listening to a story shared in the most necessary way—between two. I said I agreed with him. "After they voted him out, our last board president moved clear up to Edmonds." He laughed.

We purposely did NOT talk about the virus; this I could sense in the way we talked about anything else. But avoiding a subject and ignoring it are two different things. As we know.

For another minute, I just stood there thinking that years down the road we will look back at these months as another time in history when the fragile balance between questioning and resigning, patience and panic, freedom and restriction, had been upended.

When everything got too quiet too fast and it was too late to hide, and the world completely changed.

And with that, I waved goodbye.

I thought of popping by Trader Joe's just to see and hear other people, but I was fine with my one blessed interaction. I felt better. More balanced.

Blessed. Better. Balanced.

This makes for happiness now.

COVID DIARY

I FIND THE STRESS THE WORST of it, not knowing how things will turn out.

My friend Terri compares daily life to Groundhog Day. I say my worst fear is that I may never be able to hug people again, or touch someone's arm as I speak. We are physical people. Not touchy-feely, but affection-ately-demonstrative would describe us to a T.

We can't imagine elbow bumping.

Belltown becomes a place I've never experienced before. To begin with, there is no traffic to speak of. In all my years in this city I have never been able to cross Denny at three o'clock in the afternoon without waiting for the light.

There are no work messages in my inbox. Not one. In over a month.

Just thinking of the empty days I will have to fill and fill, while spring passes in the blink of an eye, and we just *know* how quickly summer will.

I am eating too much, thinking too much, drinking too much.

That last sentence is not just an admission but an embarrassment.

I come from a long line of women who have a deep dependency on distilled white vinegar. We love our homes to be clean, clean, clean. I add a few drops of lemon oil to mine and re-spray the counters again, vacuum again, empty the waste baskets again, everything ship-shape. While mentally I live in a mess.

If things don't improve, I will scrub the tile grout.

Really, I wonder about myself.

If you were a psychologist, you might say I clean to give myself a sense of order. If you were a nice psychologist, you might say that fussiness is a harmless coping skill. If you were an objective but truthful one, you'd say that when things get really stressful, I am detailed and meticulous. Though picky-picky-picky is probably what you had in mind.

EXCUSE ME. WHY IS LEAF BLOWING ESSENTIAL?

Larry and I bickered today. What annoys one of us about the other is magnified. We don't know exactly how to help each other right now, nor will we stop trying. This is the definition of love after all of these years.

I confess to my sister that I was stoned at her wedding and she says, "As I remember it, the most important issue on your mind was whether or not you would agree to wear panties under your dress." All this to change the subject from the dismal truth that she has had 14 patients die in the last 11 days.

When I say I don't want to spend another day trying to fit dance choreography into my living room and that Zoom does not cut it for me, creatively, she doesn't say much. If she *did* say what she was thinking, it would likely sound like this: *Jesus Christ, your troubles are nothing.*

This is why I don't share how I used to think of studio space as a Marley floor and a bank of mirrors. Or how my new studio has become a smooth section of concrete in Denny Park I share with a couple of homeless guys.

Or how I danced for the homeless guys.

Though I didn't just dance, I *performed.*

And when I was through, they clapped.

The way I see it, a performer needs to perform, so that's what I did.

I was brought up to pray at a time like this. But I've never had to deal with a time like this. And I never learned how to pray. Not really. Maybe I should have.

One more thing. My hair is falling out.

The first time I noticed way too many strands in the comb was about a week after my mother had a stroke. Left neglect they called it, "where a huge part of the disease is denial," and I remember thinking *that sounds about right,* given her skill for stumbling through life and never quite finding her footing.

Just thinking of some of the funny things my mother said in her last days gets me through these unsettled months. I rely on them now (all nice and tidy in a bullet list) because I need to laugh as much as I need food and water and counting on my work to come back.

- She wants the banana on the counter. There is no banana on the counter. But we have always come to life from entirely different realities, so I figure nothing has really changed. She sings*:* "Lu Annza the Bonanza." My sister's name is Lou Ann. My heart swells.

- Hungry as ever, she yells at the top of her lungs, "I want to go to the Outback and have a steak! With lots of mushrooms, please!"

- "I like it when you write about me. And the B I T C H." Meaning her ex-best friend who is now my father's wife.

- "Your father came to me to tell me he still loves me." What did you say, Mom? "I said it was about time." Her skin is smooth, the stress of love gone. She says really loud, "Thank you, God! I am mending the cracks."

- "I'm not dead yet. Am I?"

- "Send me a copy of your new book. Care of God."

AND STILL, WE DO

I'M LOOKING OUT MY WINDOW at a perfect summer morning: The sky is clear, with only a hint of cirrus.

Isn't it beautiful? The way the blue isn't dulled by all the sleepless nights and layers of worry.

And look! One cloud moved slightly to the left.

My saving grace has become huge appreciation of simple pleasures. I am greedy in my quest for simple pleasures. That's what I've become as of late—my very own simplicity-seeker.

The rosemary in my garden has adapted perfectly. It is doing great. It doesn't want for anything. I'm going to pop whole stalks of it into those little flasks with corks you can buy at Bartell's and fill them with olive oil—each stem suspended in time.

Only now do I realize what a great metaphor for present-day life this is.

It reminds me of the projects I used to do as a kid. Whenever family life became too stressful, out came the Crayolas. They helped. *Give me something to work with.* If nothing else, my parents' fights made me more self-reliant.

I'm thinking all this when my friend Francesca calls, sad that the *Columbus' Last Appeal to Queen Isabella* statue has been removed from the State Capitol in Sacramento. "I love that statue," she says.

She's a relatively new friend, so I don't want to say that Columbus doesn't depict a whole lot about being Italian, not to me anyway. Or how I wish that when they tear an old statue down, they will raise a cast bronze of a hard-working woman like RBG or Harriet Tubman.

And she's become a better friend since our conversation back in March when, after she had to cancel my author luncheon, she said she still wanted to be my friend.

No one has ever come right out and said this to me before. And I was surprised because all I can remember was feeling depressed that the rest of my book tour was cancelled and what could I have possibly been "so hilarious" about. When I wasn't feeling sorry for myself, I was grouchy. And when I wasn't grouchy, I was commiserating with someone else who was feeling depressed which is just another way of feeling sorry for myself and then it was time to binge on Netflix again.

All this with the collateral benefit of discovering just how easy it is to drink low-budget wine, also from Bartell's.

Francesca is pretty upset, so some other time I will tell her that her wanting to be my friend has been a high point in these low months. Tell her that it's been too long since I've made such an expressive friend, like years too long. Tell her that after I wondered aloud if maybe the government is a little too overstepping of our rights lately, and she said, "Get with the program, Maria Luisa! Human rights are so yesterday," I knew I wanted to be her friend, too. Tell her that I've been starved for our kind of conversation, and that after we talk, I always want to hug someone. "You, I guess," is what I'll say.

After we hang up, I stare at my herbal flasks. How familiar they seem even though I have never made rosemary-oil before and probably never will again.

And with *that,* it's time for a walk.

I am so happy to find one of my favorite parks (I'm not saying which one!) crowded with people gorging on sunshine.

I mean, really, the rain will be *back.*

Most people have forgotten to social distance, well, not altogether, we make a casual stab at it, but it's more like we are drawn to each other. And I *know* I'm going to be blasted for saying this, but this makes me feel *less* afraid rather than more. It's as if too much life-affirming optimism pumps through everyone's veins, and you know that nothing can restrain the course of lifeblood.

Restraint is the very antithesis of the human heart.

And we are only human, each of us.

And what are the two women next to me talking about? Nothing new, stories about their kids, the little stars of their lives. And I want to shout that it feels like we are all reaching for the stars just by being here.

The crowd is old and young and in-between. One woman holds a baby in her arms. Another sits on the grass, legs outstretched. A boy rolls up on a onewheel. Honestly, who *isn't* here among us, hoping against hope with the rest of the world.

The way we live best is like this, in fresh air and sunshine with our bodies a little closer together. And while I do (I do!) wonder if it's too risky, mostly I wonder if other people are wondering the same thing: that our nearness is like the first "time" for many of us.

We know we shouldn't.

We've been warned we shouldn't.

And still, we do.

I HAVE

WELL, IF MICHELLE OBAMA can admit to feeling blue, so will I.

At first, I didn't want to read her interview. I thought, *there are things I am not ready to rehash.*

But after reading it, I realized that it's become more than the Lurking Virus. It's that living downtown has begun to take *nerve*. It's a lot less intimidating to stay home and reorganize the closets.

But no amount of decluttering will make the latest shooting not feel like the final straw.

Again and again, the shootings. With barely a breath in between.

How slippery the edge of a neighborhood can feel.

Only blocks away, it's another world. And each new round of sirens prompts another walk up to Parsons Gardens on Highland Drive.

I know. The name of the street says it all.

But what can I say? I go there to restore myself, to breathe in the stillness, to feel the peacefulness pool around my nerve endings, the calm that comes when there is less likelihood of violence. When my friend

Raye ends our call with, "stay safe," I cannot resist the urge to say, "Easy for you to say, *you* live in Green Lake."

I envy my neighbor Amal. She is devout. She believes it's all up to Allah. I wish I could think that so I wouldn't have to wrestle with what I believe. She raises her hands to the sky, so I raise my hands to the sky. And it does make me feel better. A little. But that's the thing about *better*. It's more fleeting than *worse*.

Will the neighborhood ever bounce back?

I lose myself in work. *I* am devout at losing myself in work.

Somewhere I read that writers are preoccupied by our own competing minds, and that we can't forget that we are preoccupied. One mind just wants to *live,* while the other keeps commenting on how well, or how terribly, we are going about it.

There is so much truth to this statement. I feel it echo throughout my whole body. Really, I wish I had an X-ray of my insides twirling all over the place right now. Because while I don't believe this is the only competition within me, I do think that I've turned this mental rivalry into a sense of guidance for myself.

For instance, one of my minds knows that my friend Stephanie is, by now, sitting in our rooftop garden and that I *could* go up and bother her, while the other reminds me that this is the point of her day when she likes to stare out at Elliott Bay, smoke her cigarette, and be grateful that there is nothing more she can do about today.

Fortunately, both minds know not to interrupt her alone time.

Our rooftop has become the epitome of alone time.

But there is good news! *Kamala, when I cast my ballot, I voted for Y O U!* I mean, sorry, Joe, but vote for another man over a smarter, more capable, woman? Again?

Not. On. Your. Life.

And get this. I just heard that my first children's book will be published! I should celebrate. I will. I promise myself that I will. Because even if I haven't yet felt like celebrating the moment, I do need to celebrate the triumph.

In fact, I wish that I could have reached across the Zoom cosmos this morning to give a good long triumphant hug to one of my dance students when, mid-plié, she paused to say, "You've written a *lot* of books."

And for a while, after she said that, I did feel like celebrating.

Because I have.

A New Sense of Thanks—March 2021

IT MAY LOOK OTHERWISE to someone who has never tried, but performing is hard work. Nothing about a performance is easy. The atmosphere is focused and expectant and hyper-aware.

And no one but you is thinking about this.

And no one but you should be.

Because you, only you, must carry the room.

And if you tremble, you crash.

But once you begin you know with heat spreading through your chest warm as tile in the sun, nervous or not, that you are not going to let yourself down. You are not going to botch this. You are not going to crash.

More than anything, you want the whole evening to work.

And it does. Face-to-face, it does! All of your loose ends come together into one poised YOU.

Then the worst thing possible happens.

I woke up.

Suddenly, even the coziness of my bed seemed to belong to a previous time.

Here is what else I remember: Everyone looked happy, so happy, and my reading felt like one of many like it and, yet, what made it different was that no one recalled such an upended, lava-lamp of a time like *this*. We had forgotten all about the Coronavirus. Or never heard of it.

I could not tell which.

One woman held up a sign that read, I GAVE FEAR UP FOR LENT. It takes a strong will to laugh off fear in our time. Her knack for independence inspires. I wondered if she had come to tell *me* to stop worrying and live my life, wash my hands and be smart about contact, yes, but LIVE, and I thought maybe I should believe her.

She was only one voice, but sometimes one is enough.

I assume what you are reading into this is that I *need* one voice to be enough and you are correct.

Then, like a dream within a dream, soft solar lights come up along the aisles adding to the magic and my excitement leaps over the edge of the stage and does a cartwheel. And not one person—well, maybe there was *one* woman looking down—needs to tweet about the cartwheel to feel that they have seen it.

It was a dream, after all, a fairy tale.

I even remember wondering if the lone tweeter could hear what I was thinking: *There will always be those who repeat the mistakes of the past.* Or what the man beside her was thinking: *When bad manners become the norm, most people don't recognize it as bad anymore. But some of us do.*

He was so real, this man.

No, I am lying to you. I made him up for effect.

I suppose what I'm getting at, slowly, is that some people long for lovers the way I long to sit next to someone at a theater.

I may even want to hold their hand. It seems like the least I can do after all we've been through. I have never been remotely interested in not being close to people—I don't ever want to be *that* compliant.

So, when the day arrives, by which I mean when we come close, *closer,* let us take to the edge again, which has never been *safe.* (Although, I may be a little sorry to not have to wait in line at the grocery anymore. When that happens, I may be less apt to dress presentably.)

Let us get caught up in the thrill of live performance again, increase our level of wonder, decrease our anxiety, come fully alive.

Let us pay for theater tickets because hope is always a luxury. And just as often costly.

Let us morph into superior appreciators.

Let us thank the production staff as they welcome us back like long-lost friends.

Let us thank our lucky stars. A thousand times a day and counting.

Let us note the parallel between joy and embracing, and how one lingering hug has never been more beneficial than now.

Let us remember that the past was that. Now is *this.* And the years ahead will be altogether different. Thank goodness.

And if this anticipation is not enough to be grateful for in this new year, well, then, I do not know what gratefulness is.

Closing Thoughts

A FRIEND OF MINE CAME to dinner the other night. As soon as she arrived, she handed me a grocery bag with salad greens in it. Romaine, endive, cilantro, radicchio. "Everything looked so fresh at PCC," she said, "I over indulged."

I was thrilled to receive the vegetables, but it was the small round head of radicchio that caught my eye.

I knew this vegetable well.

And in the few minutes it took to take the vegetables out of the bag and place them in the fridge I also knew that something was triggered, but I didn't know what. I put on a smile, but my mind started to race.

The memory rose. And then I understood.

Radicchio has grown for centuries in Italy, mainly in regions in Northern Italy, especially in the Veneto region, where it still thrives. But it wasn't grown commercially in California until the early nineties. The first time I bought a head of it myself, I had just found myself in a new apartment in Seattle that was supposed to make me happy, comfort me, offer me a sense of place. And for twenty years it did that.

In every sense it was my *home*.

Now radicchio reminds me of a time in my life when I wasn't searching for a home because I had found one. And I've been thinking a lot about why we are triggered and how triggers happen in our lives before leaving us and rousing us again years later when a friend comes over with extra veggies to share.

And I don't know which affects us more, the making of the trigger, or the serendipity of its rekindling. But I'm sure that when it returns in the form of, say, red chicory, it has done so to remind that change is not only good but constant. Even if I worry I'm not up to starting over again in a new home, a new neighborhood, that I will be forever fated to be the newcomer wherever I go, and that my dream last night meant something *deep* about who I am. In my dream, I am a lone bird on a wire, separated from the safety of its flock. I couldn't imagine myself being happier alone, but I was conscious enough to feel it was true.

I should mention that this feeling made my arms flap a little.

Because I know what a privilege it is, what a luxury, to be able to simply pack up and go. We will pick a new home, four walls and a roof, and we'll move in. We will set up our treasured belongings and be nurtured by them through whatever comes next—but I know we are moving only our things, not a sense of belonging. And that I will one day soon be walking down the sidewalk and think *this isn't my home. That man living above us isn't our neighbor of twenty years. Where am I?*

In one of my early columns, I said how I could never move inland, that I need to live by the sea. This is still true. I have grown used to looking at limitlessness.

I would miss the sense of limitlessness.

I just need to move a little further north or south of downtown. Or maybe west, one of the islands connected by a ferry. Because if home is supposed to be the place where you feel you most belong, well, I have this nagging suspicion that I do not belong in Belltown any longer.

Clearly, I've had enough of the violence.

Combine that with the fact that I'm not sleeping well. Sleeplessness is a warning I listen to. When my nights are a restless toss of uncertainty, I come back to another wise saying: *nothing changes if nothing changes.*

I don't remember the exact date when I realized what was happening on the streets of our inner city, but I know for me that was the day my love of Belltown ended. I had never seen a man flail and collapse from an overdose on my way to the post office. Lots of people walked by, and lots of people did nothing. The fact of our disregard was devastating. I walked on to mail my package and wandered down to the sculpture park. I sat down on the grass.

And I knew exactly what I had to do.

When I want the best example of fatherly love, I write to Ken. We are always eager to bring each other up-to-date. "The best life consists of a series of little lives," he wrote back. And this is how relieved I was to read his email: I shutdown my laptop. Next came the tears. I think it is amazing how well our innate reflexes work. A good cry heals.

So here's what I think. Our city is not alone. I am not alone. Our whole country is struggling with the question *where do we go from here?* We are all trying to learn from the choices we have made and will make.

And if I want a view of where my own decisions have led me, I can just look out of my window at my next little life to see every little thing I am supposed to.

Acknowledgements

So much appreciation for the support I receive from the team at Chatwin Books. "Thank you" doesn't begin to express the gratefulness I feel. When people believe in you, support your work, it is so much easier to be a more open person and a more candid writer.

To my blessed first readers (even if you had no idea that's what you were doing)—my friends, my confidants: Sheila, Ken, Lou Ann, Salina, Harriet, Lynette, Camille, Larry, Phil, Stephanie. I needed your outlook while writing this book, I needed *you*. More than you know.

The essays in this collection began as monthly columns and are the chronological stories of my life as I remember them; I have changed a few names of my friends to ensure their privacy.

A special thank you to the generous editors I have had the pleasure of working with, Debbi Lester, Christy Korrow, Vera M. Chan, Jessica Keller, Christina O'Conner, and long-time radio producer who never made me feel like my mistakes in the booth were mistakes at all, Ed Bremer.

I would like to thank the following publications and radio stations where many of these essays first appeared, some in slightly different form.

The Seattle Times; *Weekend Edition*, National Public Radio; *Dance Teacher* magazine; *Seattle MET*; *City Living* magazine; *Seattle Post Intelligencer*; *Queen Anne & Magnolia News*; *Art Access*; *Honolulu Star-Advertiser*; *Lilipoh*; *Grief Digest Magazine*; *A Network for Grateful Living*; *GoNOMAD Travel* magazine; *GNU Journal*; *We The Italians*; *Lights: A Literary Journal*; *Raven Chronicles*; GFWC Newsletter; *Peninsula Daily News*; *The Port Townsend & Jefferson County Leader*; *The Oregonian*; *Casual Uncluttering*; KSER, FM; KONP, AM.

Several of these essays, as they really happened, were inspiration for my first novel.

And possibly a second.

In the hopes that the determined novel-writing-woman who wrote the first one pushes me in that direction.

I would love for this to happen.

But the single-minded writer I was then, well, on her behalf I am trying to get her away from her desk a little more often to delight in other possibilities.

If, indeed, there *are* other possibilities.

For someone like her.

A Note About Context

This memoir in essays begins after a rather embarrassing New Year's Eve party where I had a little too much fun. Obama was still in office, his second term, and the focus of life for many of us had not yet become how uneasy it makes us feel to thoroughly mistrust someone elected to the highest office of our country.

That, of course, was eye-opening.

So, it's not surprising that the tone is a little more light-hearted at first. Until even the most personal reflections begin to relate to public issues that arose: immigration, opioid addiction, Me Too, homophobia, prejudice, religious zealousness, homelessness, preparedness, the illusion of "staying safe," and the question every citizen should struggle with once their democracy is threatened: *where do we go from here?*

The collection ends in the spring of 2021 after the word "Corona" became the panic of our lives, saying it, hearing it, *feeling* it, each and every moment of every single day. When sheltering-in-place became a good reason to refine these essays. So, in quiet seclusion—in keeping with what I need and who I am—I put off all thoughts of tomorrow and dug in.

Lucky for me, writing has always made me feel less sheltered from the world, alone with my ideas and fears (except the process of writing overrides my fear), but never as lonely as, say, when I'm in a room full of people and I can't think of a thing to say.

And all the intimate things—insights, memories, reactions, joys, difficulties—that occurred along the way are nothing, really, compared to the worldly events that confront us, but they are *my* nothings.

So naturally, I wrote about them.

Actually, I unwound in them.

My hope is that you will, too.